Fighting Together

Encouraging Marriages to Fight Together
Instead of Each Other

CORNELIUS & HEATHER LINDSEY

Dedication

We dedicate this book to our beautiful children, Logan and Taylor Lindsey. We pray that this book plants seeds in our current generation for your generation. We pray that your marriages and your generation's marriages are healthy, strong and equally yoked. We pray away any ungodly, distracting and confusing relationships right now in the name of Jesus. Your generation will be led by the Holy Spirit and you will see great examples in our generation for you all to follow as you follow Jesus.

Mama & Daddy love you so much.

Table of Contents

Chapter 4

Chapter 5

Chapter 6

Chapter 7

Chapter 8

Chapter 9

Chapter 10

Chapter 11

Chapter 12

Chapter 13

Chapter 14

Bonus Chapter

Introduction

We are not marriage experts whatsoever, but our marriage is very unique. As soon as we got married, we stepped into full time ministry, and this took a huge toll on us. Now, nine years later, we have two beautiful babies, and manage an international ministry and a growing church in Atlanta, GA. We don't say these things to qualify us, we just want you to know that no matter how long you've been married, you can use your story to help someone.

We've witnessed such an attack against marriages in this generation and it has been heavy on our hearts to write a book about fighting together. In our parent's generations, it seemed like people stayed together for forty and fifty years and worked through everything. Now, it seems like we give up too quickly, throw away things too fast, and we refuse to endure. We are quick to think the grass is greener somewhere else, doing something else, while blaming our spouse as if we married the wrong person.

We want you to know that it's all a lie from the pit of hell. Satan desires to sift your marriage, to confuse it, to make you think that you're better off without it. Well we came to tell you that the grass is as green as your perspective. Our hope is that you and your spouse will read this book together in order to stop fighting one another, and start fighting FOR each other.

Chapter 1

The Spiritual Fight

I sat in my closet and balled my eyes out. My husband and I just got in a really bad argument—the worst we've ever had. Even though we had only been married for seven months at this point, I was finished. I screamed, "I AM NOT DOING THIS ANYMORE!" Sitting in that small closet in Mississippi, I tried to figure out my exit plan: "I could go next door and stay in a hotel, but we don't have any money in our account. I could move back to New York and get a better job! I will get an apartment somewhere and move on with my life. Nobody would even know, our marriage will fade away and people won't even notice.

We didn't have a ministry or a following then, and I literally had one friend in Mississippi. Would I be embarrassed about leaving? Maybe for a season, but then everyone would forget and we would move on. In the midst of my overthinking, I heard the Holy Spirit say, *"Heather, this is a spiritual fight."* What, Lord? He continued, *"I didn't change my mind about your marriage because you're going through a rough patch. I am still right here with you. I know it's hard, but there's something on the other side of this. Stop fighting each other, I want you to fight together."*

"God, please. I'm sorry! I married this crazy man and he doesn't even listen to me! Did you HEAR what he just said to me?!"

As I continued to cry out to the Lord, He began to show me my part. He showed me that I continuously nag and complain. He told me that I think I'm perfect and I look down on my husband. He showed me that I have unfair expectations of my marriage and that I wasn't allowed to quit on the process.

In the midst of my tears, my husband calls me into the other room while he was on the phone with our mentoring pastor. He gave us this scripture:

"But there is one thing I want you to know:
The head of every man is Christ, the head of
woman is man, and the head of Christ is
God."— 1 Corinthians 11:3

He gave us an image of me and my husband's heads being cut off spiritually. If I'm headless, where does my head go? My head goes to our future children, and my husband's head goes where mine once was. Since my husband is headless, his head comes from Christ. Christ's head comes from God. Because my husband and I are one *flesh* (Mark 10:8), his head wouldn't intentionally try to hurt my body because it's his body too. I wouldn't rebel against my own head—my body would submit to the head of it's physical body. What a perspective that we hadn't seen before! When I looked at my husband, I saw Christ. Since I submit as *unto* the Lord, I do it for GOD, not for my husband. He will have good and bad days, but as long as I am submitting as unto Jesus, my perspective is changed.

I would do **anything** for Jesus! He died for me! He brings me back when I am at my worst. My husband? I would do anything for him too, but he's my husband, not my Lord. My husband can really make me mad and in the midst of those good and bad feelings, I may try to justify why, "I ain't submitting today." You see the difference? I am no longer submitting as unto my husband, but as unto Jesus Christ.

> *"For our struggle is not against flesh and blood, but against the rulers, against the powers, against the world forces of darkness, against the spiritual forces of wickedness in the heavenly places."—Ephesians 6:20*

If you're fighting in your marriage, I want you to know that these tests and trials are pruning and preparing you for what He has called your marriage to do. I'm encouraging you to not quit on your marriage and to work through issues as the Holy Spirit leads you. I know your spouse may not deserve it, but I'm reminded of John 3:16, *"For God loved the world so much that he gave his one and only Son, so that everyone who believes in him will not perish but have eternal life."* That's a type of love that is completely selfless. We did not deserve the sacrifice of Jesus Christ, but He still redeemed us from the curse of the Law and set us free from the pit of hell. Through and by His sacrifice, we became citizens of heaven with an expectation of spending eternity with Him. We didn't deserve it, but He granted it to us anyway. Hallelujah!

I wonder what would have happened if *we quit on our marriage that day.* What would I be doing? I definitely wouldn't be preaching with a worldwide ministry. We wouldn't have our church. We wouldn't have our children, Logan and Taylor. *We would have allowed selfishness to ruin the call on our lives.* We would have missed the calling and mission of our marriage because we decided to give up spiritually.

What do I mean by spiritually? Well, we are spirits that live in physical bodies and we possess a soul.

"For God is Spirit, so those who worship him must worship in spirit and in truth."—*John* 4:24

If we are going to worship God in spirit, then we need to surrender our marriages to Him. We have to allow the Holy Spirit to transform us into His image based on

Romans 12:2, by refusing to conform to this world's thoughts on how our marriage should be.

What does this world say about marriage? It's often referred to as an old and outdated institution; considered unnecessary and "just a piece of paper;" replaceable and temporary; no headship and no God.

What does God say about marriage? His idea (Genesis 2:24); His purpose (Genesis 2:18); To bring glory to Him (Ephesians 5:31-32); Two taking on ten thousand (Deuteronomy 32:30); Be fruitful and multiply (Genesis 1:28); Submission as unto Christ (Ephesians 5:22-24); representation of Christ and the Church (Ephesians 5:25-31).

It's important that as believers, we spend less time studying dresses, venues, and décor for the event of a wedding, and more time studying the scriptures to learn and understand biblical marriage.

I used to think that marriage was going to be all about me: "Here are my love languages (*The Five Love Languages*, by Gary Chapman) and you better love me the way I want to receive love and do everything to make me happy. When I cook and clean, and I'm a great wife you better tell me how great of a wife I am to you.

It was selfish and rooted in making *me* feel good. My love was conditional and based on how my husband treated me. One day the Holy Spirit captured my heart, "Heather, do you do what you do because you love Me and Cornelius, or do you do it for praise from your husband?"

"Lord, you already know my answer. I do it because I want my husband to tell me how great I am. It's completely conditional."

How flesh-driven is that perspective? I am reminded of Matthew 5:24:

"If you are kind only to your friends, how are you different from anyone else? Even pagans do that."

We have a responsibility to love those who don't always treat us the way we want to be treated. Our love shouldn't be based on a condition. We should love without ceasing because that is how Christ loves us.

I want to be different than this world. I don't want my marriage to be like what I see on TV, in magazines, or even in my family. I want my own marriage and to find what works for *us*. I want our marriage to be this beautiful secret place where we trust each other and we walk by faith together. Where we build each other up and we don't tear one another down.

Your marriage won't be your oasis from this world if you are constantly doing everything you do for the wrong reasons. We serve our spouses, we love unconditionally, and we support each other because we love our partner and we love God.

The Spiritual Fight

I can recall a time when we got in another really bad disagreement. I mean, it was rough! Not as bad as the closet fight, but it was pretty bad. We have a rule that says we won't sleep in separate beds, no matter how bad the disagreement. So I'm laying in the bed, kicking covers and putting pillows between us because I didn't want him to touch me. *I was heated!* I knew that the bible says not to let the sun go down on your wrath, but I didn't care. *He needed to be glad that I was even sleeping in the same bed with him.* As I drifted off to sleep, I had a dream where I saw a dozen devil like gremlins running in circles around our bed. I looked down at them, then asked the Lord in my dream, "What are they?" Their faces were disfigured and as I stared at them, the Lord answered me, "Heather, those are demons sent to ruin your marriage. They have been assigned to bring division, strife, and confusion in your home."

WHAT? Oh heck no.

I'm fighting back! There is **no** way that I am going to let these gremlins come up in my home and ruin our life! I woke up quickly, woke up my husband, and apologized for going to bed mad and for our disagreement. I refused to let the enemy come in and ruin my marriage. There was no way. I jumped up, grabbed some olive oil and started to anoint our bed, our bedroom door and the entryway of our home. I casted out any demonic or satanic attack, I not only casted them out but I told those little demons to go back to hell where they belong. I decided not to give satan an open door into my marriage that day.

> "Stay alert! Watch out for your great enemy,
> the devil. He prowls around like a roaring
> lion, looking for someone to devour."—1 Peter
> 5:8

He's roaring. He's looking. He longs to divide and cause confusion. This is why it's important that you are spending time with the Holy Spirit so you can recognize that this battle isn't against flesh and blood, but against principalities and unseen things.

You may feel like your spouse isn't saved, or where you are spiritually, and if this is the case, you have the opportunity to win them over with your quiet and gentle spirit And, guys, this works for you too! I have watched my husband win me over by refusing to fuss and fight with me. You can't force God onto your spouse because when they signed up to marry you, that wasn't a requirement. Forcing God on them will only create resentment and thoughts of you being "better than them." Instead, win them over by being patient, kind, and prayerful. Pray that God uncovers their eyes so that they can see the truth. Your spouse is not a "project" or your "experiment." You're not his mama and he isn't your daddy. No one wants to feel like they're being spoken down to or that they're less than.

The Spiritual Fight

Realize that you and your spouse are involved in a spiritual fight for your marriage right now. Fight back with the Word of God! Exchange what the enemy is saying to you about your spouse and your marriage with what God says. When you're being told to go to the courts and get a divorce, reflect that fiery dart of the enemy with your shield of faith (Ephesians 6:10-16). Then, strike him with the words of God. Remind Satan that although Moses permitted divorce, it was never meant to be that way (Matthew 19:8). Remind him that God hates divorce (Malachi 2:16), and that he's defeated and unable to control you or your marriage.

It's time to fight back! It's time for both of you to fight spiritually for your marriage by praying together, building each other up, and by staying spiritually alert to combat the advances of the enemy with the Word of God.

Chapter 2

Your Marriage Story

Every marriage is different, but your marital issues are not uncommon. My wife and I had to learn this early on in our marriage. It can be easy to feel as if your marriage should mirror everyone else's; easy to get caught up in trying to keep up with everyone else; easy to think the issues in your marriage are isolated to only your marriage and no other couple has issues like yours. This was our story.

Heather and I began our marriage thinking that every other couple was perfect. We would sit down with couples on double dates hoping we could relate to them somehow, but that never happened. They almost always appeared perfect and polished, *while we knew we were not.* In fact, we probably argued the entire car ride to the restaurant. I would slam my car door, and she would walk ahead of me in an act of defiance, but we put on our smiles to save face in front of the couples we were meeting. We would sit down and endure an hour of conversation and acting like we actually liked one another—leaving feeling worse than when we came. We thought our marriage was destined to fail because of our problems. We felt isolated. We felt unheard. We felt alone.

One night, we sat down with a couple who were both lawyers and, like us, were newly married with no children. Heather and I had just finished arguing before walking into the restaurant. We were upset with each other because we were failing to meet one another's expectations. After conversing with the couple for about thirty minutes, the husband got up and went to the restroom. I went to the car to grab my phone and when I came back to the table, Heather and the other woman were having a serious conversation. I could tell from the look on my wife's face that whatever was being said was intense and the other wife was crying hysterically.

I questioned what I just walked in on but Heather told me to speak with her husband. He walked back to the table from the restroom with a look of disgust on his face. He couldn't believe that his wife broke down in front of us. After calming her down we finally started to get to the root of their issue. They, like us, felt their marriage was falling apart. They felt like everything they were building was worthless and, like us, felt all alone. We were able to share our own struggles in our marriage, including the argument we had on the way there. They felt relieved since they had also argued the entire way to the dinner. We started to really relate with one another and the mask of perfection was ripped away, allowing us to expose ourselves, our faults, and our marital problems to provide hope and encouragement to each other.

It is important for you and your spouse to realize that your issues are not new. Heather and I have argued and said things that we regret many times. I have been so angry that I've punched walls, broke lamps, and stormed out of the house. My wife and I had an argument so bad that I stopped the car on the side of a busy intersection, jumped out, and started walking down the street without a clue as to where I was going. I've used words against her that I regret, as she has with me. Our marriage has been far from perfect, and we finally got to a point where we were consistently willing to work towards perfection. We had to realize that our marital issues weren't uncommon.

There was one argument where we both went below the belt by saying things we knew were off limits, but we didn't care. We were hurt, and we were looking to hurt each other. We were both frustrated with one another: I wanted my wife to do more around the house, and she wanted me to be more affectionate. After almost an hour of belittling one another, Heather went into the bedroom and slammed the door, which is something I hate. I went to the door and threatened to take it off the hinges.

I knew I needed to calm down so I sat down and was immediately confronted with these verses:

Fighting Together

"So husbands ought to love their own wives
as their own bodies. He who loves his own
wife loves himself; for no one ever hated his
own flesh, but nourishes and cherishes it, just
as Christ also does the church, because we
are members of His body."—Ephesians 5:28-30

I was immediately convicted by those words. I was not following them at all. It was in that moment that I needed to learn that every destructive word I spoke about my wife was destroying me too. I had to realize that my words, which were born out of hurt and frustration, were damaging our marriage. It was like I was taking a sledgehammer and hammering away at the foundation we were building. Instead of edifying my wife, I was tearing her down! I was so ashamed. I didn't know it at the time, but my wife was in the bedroom, and she later told me that she was convicted by these words:

"Love is patient, love is kind and is not
jealous; love does not brag and is not
arrogant, does not act unbecomingly; it does
not seek its own, is not provoked, does not
take into account a wrong suffered, does not
rejoice in unrighteousness, but rejoices with
the truth; bears all things, believes all things,
hopes all things, endures all things."—1
Corinthians 13:4-7

I could hear her sobbing as I approached our bedroom door. I walked in and hugged her and told her how much I loved her. I asked for forgiveness for my lack of patience and anger and she asked for forgiveness as well. We both knew we had work to do in our marriage, but that moment cemented the fact that we were committed to receiving correction from the Lord and fighting together!

We've learned that it's important to be open to receive correction as the Holy Spirit gives it to you. He will guide you in all truth and teach the words of Christ, which is written in John 16:13. Depend on Him to correct you or reach out to trusted advisors to mediate the argument between you and your spouse. We've also learned that reading 1 Corinthians 13:4-7 out loud in the middle of an argument works well for us. Reading the Word will help the both of you gain perspective. After reading it, pray together.

Well, what if my spouse doesn't want to hear the Word or won't pray with me? We suggest you go away to read it and pray for you and your spouse. Don't continue to provoke your spouse or to be provoked yourself. Remember that what you do to your spouse is ultimately what you are doing to yourself because the two of you are one.

My wife and I sit with many couples all the time, and it can be difficult to listen to the problems they are facing. It can be hard to watch the tears fall and to see the emotional separation between them, but they are encouraged when they hear my wife and I tell them about our issues. Allowing them to see another couple that goes through, or has gone through, the same thing is refreshing. It lets them know that they aren't alone, and that there is hope and reconciliation on the other side of their struggle.

Your marriage is important. In fact, generations after you are depending on the success of it. You might believe it isn't special because of the problems your marriage has faced, but you cannot allow the presence of a couple of weeds to blind you of the presence of your beautiful garden. Maybe you believe your spouse is not "the one" God wanted you to marry. Maybe you think you made a mistake. Well, there is great wisdom found in Deuteronomy 22:10 that tells us never to yoke an ox with a donkey. The ox is considered a clean, submissive beast, where as the donkey is viewed as unclean, rebellious, and stubborn. Spiritually, the Jews were considered to be the ox, while the donkey represented the Gentiles, which was once you and me. The Gentiles were kept behind the veil until Jesus Christ ripped it down. He became the passage for us to gain entrance to the Father. We now boldly approach the throne of Grace because of His sacrifice. Hallelujah! There no longer remains a separation between the Jews and the Gentiles, the Romans and the Greeks. We are now one body in Jesus Christ.

Your Marriage Story

What is special about this is that the ox and donkey don't have to be muzzled together; instead, Jesus has transformed the very nature of the donkey into a submissive ox. Now the two submissive, clean beasts can plow the field together. You may read that and think, "Well, that's nice and all, but I still feel like I'm an ox dragging my spouse through life." Perhaps your spouse has become stubborn to the things of God, stale in his or her maturity; as if he or she has stopped trying to do anything more with his or her life.

It's the marriage where communication has all but ceased, and intimacy is nonexistent. It is where one of you is constant and consistent in attending church, reading the Scriptures, giving regularly, and praying daily, but your spouse has all but stopped everything. It is where one spouse is continuing to grow while the other has fallen back. Many believe this scenario entitles the maturing spouse to leave the one that has fallen behind, but please understand that this does not mean your marriage is over. *The same Christ that changed the nature of the unclean, rebellious donkey can change your spouse.* Your focus is to pray fervently for the change in your spouse and yourself. Your mission is to be so loving and encouraging that you win him or her over with your love.

Please understand that your marriage story will be different from everyone else's, and that is okay. Maybe your story had a rocky start, or the two of you started with a child before getting married. Maybe you and your spouse had an abortion, one of you had the other sent to jail, your parents or family members don't want the two of you to get married, or you and your spouse couldn't afford a ceremony or a honeymoon. Does this mean your marriage is destined to fail? Absolutely not! The world would love for you to think that this means your marriage is over. That is a lie from the pit of hell. God restores! He specializes in taking what was broken and thrown away by the world and making it new. He takes broken vessels and molds them until He is ready to present them as He pleases.

What's amazing about our restoring God is that He doesn't just return the broken vessel to its original state like we do with our broken items. *No, He remolds it in such a way that the broken vessel returns in greater condition than it was before.* When He puts His hands on it the value increases dramatically. Imagine what would happen if you fell on your face and prayed that God would touch your marriage—restoring everything that's broken and straightening everything that's crooked. Do you believe He can do it? Do you have faith that He can change your marriage story? Do you have faith that your future together is brighter than the thoughts of divorce today? *If so, put this book down, find your quiet place, and cry out to God.* Boldly and confidently approach the King of Kings and Lord of Lords and ask that He place His hand on your marriage. Pray that Jehovah Rapha—He who heals, restores, and delivers—will heal your marriage physically, emotionally, and spiritually. Meditate on Psalm 6:2-3. Repent of your own wrongdoing. Recognize that God forgives you once you ask for it, and know that God will restore the years you've lost by pouring so much joy in your heart that you forget the years you've wasted. After praying, join a community of faith that can hold you accountable, encourage you, and pray fervently for you. Go ahead and put the book down and pray, and return once you've finished.

If you took advantage of that time of prayer, please know that my wife and I add our faith with yours. Your marriage has purpose. It has meaning. It has substance! Your marriage story of redemption and restoration is worth telling the world about. Allow God to use your story to encourage and challenge others. Some marriage somewhere can benefit from your marriage testimony, so don't hide it—allow God to get the glory out of your marriage. It is your testimony, and no one can live your truth like the both of you. Work at living your story out together because you are more valuable together than you are apart. You can fight with greater accuracy and strength when you are together.

Wherever you are in your story right now, whether struggling or restored, that isn't the end of it. You might just be finishing up chapter one. The final chapter has yet to come, so live with the idea that you and your spouse are going to write a story worth emulating! Do it all for the glory of God. Hallelujah! Hallelujah! Hallelujah!

Chapter 3

Purpose in Marriage

A husband who had been married for two years came to me and explained that he was bored with his marriage. He said that he and his wife were merely existing, they didn't have fun anymore, and he missed the times they shared when they were courting. I've heard this same scenario many times from many couples but for some reason they always forget that their marriage has a purpose beyond just existing together. Marriage is more than just sex, trying to enjoy one another for a few hours on the weekend, and trying to see all of your family from both sides on holidays. Both of you have purpose, and that purpose is to come together to glorify God.

As singles, you and your spouse were like two free-flowing ships floating in the ocean. As believers, you were headed towards the same lighthouse, Jesus. He is the captain of your ships and He didn't leave the two of you helpless or hopeless. He provided Holy Spirit, to guide you along the path. He takes hold of the wheel and lifts the anchor. The two of you were headed in the same direction, unaware of one another. As the both of you continued to head towards the lighthouse, you meet and the courting begins, engagement follows, and marriage becomes the reality. There's so much excitement during the courting process because it's fun to learn new things about one another and explore the possibilities of the future. The journey to the altar seems exciting and exhilarating, but too often the excitement dies away after the couple has said, 'I do.'

What does the bible say about the purpose of marriage?

According to the Bible, our purpose, the reason we are here, is for God's glory. Because God sees us as one flesh (Mark 10:8), He expects that everything we do, including our marriage, bring glory to Him. In other words, our purpose is to praise God, worship Him, and to accomplish His will on this earth. This is what glorifies Him; therefore, in this we find that God has given us a reason and meaning for our existence. We were created by Him, according to his desire, and our lives are to be lived for Him so that we might accomplish what he has for us to do.

Before Heather and I were married, we discussed our purpose as individuals. My wife believed she was purposed to reach broken women and share the Gospel with them in hopes they would be changed and transformed. She wanted to share her story to encourage women through life. I told her that I believed I was purposed to preach the Gospel to the lost and broken. I explained that I was purposed to pastor a church and to run for political office. The last one has yet to materialize, but only God knows what the future will bring. We shared our purposes with one another, then we discussed how they were to align so we could fulfill them in our marriage.

The sole purpose for us as Christians is to glorify God with our lives by living with a holy standard and fulfilling the Great Commission. That does not only include preaching behind a podium! It includes loving our spouse when we don't think they deserve it, being patient with our children, being kind to in laws that we don't think deserve it and so much more!

After having a discussion with one couple about their purpose together, they decided to get serious about their marriage. The wife was the owner of a bakery, while her husband was a corporate accountant, and they both believed they were fulfilling the purpose God gave them. During our conversation, the wife expressed a need to get the bakery's finances in order. She was weak in that area and unsurprisingly, that was her husband's strength. Isn't it funny how God does that? After looking over the bakery's finances, they decided to bring their strength's together to glorify God with their marriage and their business—the husband quit his job to be the bakery's full-time accountant. They began fulfilling their purposes together and it was beautiful to see.

After coming together on the mission of their marriage, they realized that they needed to fulfill their commission as believers so they opened their bakery for bible study twice a week, which created an environment for discipleship. They placed verses on the bottom of the cupcake sheets, left pamphlets about their faith next to the register, and painted verses on the wall. There was no doubt they were believers. After about a year, they were still successfully progressing in their marriage and business. Their marriage was stronger than ever now that they spent their days with one another and were building something worthwhile together.

My wife and I drafted a purpose statement at the beginning of our marriage. It read 'Our purpose is to gather people together to have the Word of God taught to them, that they may grow by what they hear, and be challenged to go into the world to fulfill their Gospel Commission.' That purpose has stuck with us since it's origin as we both lead ministries that seek to empower men and women to fulfill their God given callings.

Starting our marriage with a clear understanding of what we were brought together by God to do gave us direction and something to always come back to when we get distracted from our purpose by everyday life. If your marriage didn't start with a clear mission, define one now. Make it plain to your spouse what you feel God has called you to do, and how you both can come together to manifest one another's strengths. If you have yet to identify those things, seek Holy Spirit's guidance in defining what that looks like for you individually and in your marriage.

What we do doesn't come from how we feel, but from who we are. We are Christians; therefore, our lives should reflect our faith. Our businesses and how we give reflects our faith, along with every other aspect of our lives. The same must be true for you and your spouse. Consider what the two of you are doing and ask yourselves if it glorifies God, fulfills the Gospel Commission, or brings your purposes together. Take time to sit down and discuss the purpose statement for your household.

The purpose statement allows for the both of you to know where you are headed, how you're going to get there, and who's going to be glorified in the process. To exist without purpose or vision is to wander with no destination in sight. Having a purpose statement written down gives your marriage direction and removes distraction. Heather and I are approached by television shows, interview opportunities, speaking engagements, and many more public opportunities, but we deny most of it *because we know it goes against our purpose.* Most of it doesn't glorify God, so we cannot support it. We refer back to our purpose statement to make sure everything we do keeps us on the path we're supposed to be on. It can do the same for you.

The two of you are purposed to populate the world with generations of Christians. This is why you train your children in the truth and admonition of the Lord. Marriage is the proper place for sex, provides great companionship, gives shelter and protection for your children, and paints a beautiful picture between Christ and the Church. You both must realize the importance of your marriage, and you can never allow anyone to tell you otherwise.

Chapter 4

Learning to Trust Your Spouse

I saw a very healthy marriage in my parents. They were married for almost 40 years before my dad passed away when I was 17 years old. I didn't grow up around a lot of screaming and fussing, so I can say I had a pretty good upbringing.

Even though I had a stable example, I was afraid of marriage for many years. I desired to get married but when I met someone, I would tear them apart in my head and come up with reasons why I couldn't marry them. I can even recall telling one guy not to propose to me.

Forever?

"Like, wait, I have to submit to you forever? Like, for the rest of my life? What if I don't like you anymore? I have to stick it out?"

I thought this way until I met my husband, Cornelius. I had peace, I respected him, I believed in him, and I looked up to him since the beginning of our courtship. I felt like there was nothing we couldn't accomplish together. I thought that my fears had melted away and that we would skip off in the wind forever, *but that proved to be a lie.*

In the first couple years of our marriage, I couldn't stomach when my husband grew silent. He had this thing where if the Lord was dealing with him about something heavy or if he was stressed out about something, he would go inward. He would silently try to figure out what he would do and he wouldn't be able to articulate to me what was frustrating him. This drove me up the wall.

I had a worker mentality where I felt like I needed to earn my husband's love and approval. I was always afraid that he would abandon me or leave our marriage, which I later discovered was rooted in deeper abandonment issues from me being adopted. When he grew silent because of ministry frustrations, I would assume that he was mad at me, when most times it had nothing to do with me. I would try to do all of these things to make him feel better but then I would get frustrated with him for even being upset, which made him mad because I wasn't being understanding of his current season.

As I vented to the Lord, "Holy Spirit! I need your help. I don't understand this man that you created!" The

Holy Spirit said to me, *"Heather, I know Cornelius. I created him. Will you trust me concerning him?"*

"You mean to tell me that you can actually give me specific instructions on how to make my marriage work?"

Why haven't I been acknowledging you in this Lord?

"In all your ways acknowledge him, and he will make straight your paths."—Proverbs 3:6

At what point did you stop acknowledging the Lord concerning your marriage? Even in small things? That scripture says in ALL of your ways. Not, part of your ways, on some of the days you feel like it, or when you think your spouse deserves it.

God created each of you and purposed you together. He alone can show you how to make your marriage great for His glory.

I believe it is in our nature to allow our flesh to respond and not the Holy Spirit concerning our spouses. We allow our past to respond for us. We allow the opinions of mama and them to respond, but not the Holy Spirit. We allow thoughts like, "How dare my spouse? They don't deserve me!"

The Holy Spirit had to show me that I am very critical and harsh of my husband. He showed me that my husband often feels like I talk down to him, and how can your spouse open up to you if they don't feel safe in their marriage? My husband would shut down because he felt the weight of leadership, of feeling purposeless, and other feelings that I probably couldn't even articulate for him. I actually thought that I could fix those things that were going on in his heart.

But you cannot fix your spouse. They are not a science project. Our issues are spiritual and much deeper than anything that we can physically see.

"For we are not fighting against flesh-and-blood enemies, but against evil rulers and authorities of the unseen world, against mighty powers in this dark world, and against evil spirits in the heavenly places."—
Ephesians 6:12

The Lord showed me that I need to stop nagging him and give him a chance to open up. He reminded me that we are on the same team, but most times we act like we are against one another.

I would compare my husband's walk with the Lord to my walk. I spent hours and hours before the Lord and I would roll my eyes at my husband's prayer time because I didn't feel like he was as zealous as me. I was so unfair and self-righteous our first year of marriage. I had a list of things that I felt like he could do better and I was afraid of totally trusting that our marriage could survive because of my unrealistic expectations. I didn't even give my husband a chance to grow into the man I prayed for; instead, I told him who he needed to be in order for me to be happy.

Of course we didn't trust each other! Although my husband had his issues, the Lord showed me that I must focus on Him and allow for Him to change me from the inside out. To this day, I am intentional about changing the only person I can change, me.

Some of you may even be mad at your spouse because they won't read this book with you. You want so bad for your marriage to work and you want things to change, but you cannot force your spouse to do anything. *Your power is in prayer.* Your power is showing by example. You get the book, read it and apply it. Then, your spouse will see the positive changes you are making and may be more OPEN to change. As you read this book, let the Holy Spirit change *you* and your spouse! I have watched my prayers for my husband come to pass over and over again. We cannot give up on praying and trusting in the Lord!

Are you trying to change your spouse or do you trust that the Holy Spirit can mold them into the person that God called them to be? I have learned that I am better off stepping back and letting the Holy Spirit make my husband into His image. If I would finally shut up, my husband can grow into the leader that I've dreamed about, but it won't happen with me complaining and nagging him every day.

Fighting Together

"Heather, you don't understand what my spouse has done to hurt me!"

I know that they hurt you but one day we are going to be judged on our *response to the hurt.* I know it's painful and difficult to look past that hurt but I'm confident Jesus feels the same way when we reject His pleas for our full trust. He freely forgave us. He freely chose us. He freely gave us an option to choose Him. He freely saved us. If Jesus Himself doesn't force us to change, why do we want to change our spouses?

The question is, do you trust God to change your spouse?

I think that if we are honest, we fear truly letting go in our marriage and completely trusting 100%. If you're like me, you've been hurt in the past, rejected, ignored, and physically abused in relationships. I came with a lot of baggage and it was really hard for me to put all of my eggs in one basket, even after "I do."

Fear is caused by the belief that someone or something is dangerous or a threat to us or our way of life.

What does the bible say about fear?

"For God has not given us a spirit of fear, but of power and of love and of a sound mind."—
2 Timothy 1:7 (NKJV)

Learning to Trust Your Spouse

We have to remember that the person God assigned us to **is not out to get us**. We have to confront that fear in our heart. Even if you feel like your spouse isn't for you, believe the best until you physically see it. I felt like Cornelius wasn't for me, but all along he really was! I charged my husband for the hurt from my past because I thought that he was going to hurt me like others had before him.

Get to the root of your fears and confront the painful memories that birthed them. You have to let the Holy Spirit break those soul ties from your past. You are married now and you are no longer soul-tied to your exes, or your family who may have hurt you. Don't bring that mess into your marriage. Satan would love to make you compare your marriage to your past, birthing fear and causing you to wonder whether the grass was greener. Let's clear up something really quick: it isn't. Everything you need for the perfect will of God for your life is found in your covenant of marriage. Thankfully, anyone who hurt you in the past is not included in that equation. Rebuke that fear that says you married the wrong person. No, you married your spouse, you believe in them and you are willing to work out life wit them.

The crazy thing is this, if you even look back at that past relationship before your spouse, there is a reason the relationship ended! This is what Satan does to cause confusion, he tries to make you believe that the grass was greener in your past but it's just a mirage. A false picture. Instead, block your exes phone number, remove them from social media, hide their posts or whatever it takes to be free from those feelings. You may need to get rid of all of that stuff that they gave you. Whatever you need to do to be free, let the Holy Spirit lead you. Many times, soul ties aren't discussed after you're married but I wonder how many ex relationships illegally stood next to you on your wedding day from your past, ready to ruin your marriage.

How do you break them?

Declare this with me:

I declare in the name of Jesus that every single soul tie that I have picked up along the way, whether it be from a relationship, from pornography, from a ungodly friendship—I declare that that spirit is broken off of me right now in the name of Jesus. It will no longer affect my marriage. My marriage will be successful and we will walk by faith! My marriage will survive! My marriage is not like anybody else's marriage, and I will guard my heart and continue to believe the best!

In Jesus' Name, Amen.

(Now, if you are in a physically abusive marriage, we 100% recommend separation and safety while you both go through counseling and work on allowing the Holy Spirit to help you.)

Chapter 5

Healing your Marriage

Do you remember your wedding day? With tears in your eyes and a joy in your face, you promised these vows to God, and your spouse: "I take thee to be my lawfully wedded, to have and to hold, from this day forward, for better or for worse, for richer, for poorer, in sickness and in health, to love and to cherish, and I promise to be faithful to you until death parts us." You would have promised *whatever* it took because you were so in love that day!

Did you know then that those vows would get tested in the midst of your marriage? Regardless of what has happened up to this point, I believe that the same God that heals physical bodies can heal a marriage. At times, we as Christians are so surprised when our marriage gets attacked! We almost expect our lives to get attacked in every other way but not in our marriages. I believe that the enemy seeks to destroy the marriage first because if he can disarm the guardians of the home then he has access to the children, then the community, then the state, then the nation. It's a pattern of destruction and we must recognize that Satan is on the prowl, looking for a marriage to dismantle. We must constantly be aware of his tactics and positioned to dispute his lies with the Word of God.

Have you and your spouse ever gotten into a really huge fight over something? I mean, to the point where you started to pack your bags to leave? Well that has happened to us before and in those disagreements we have said some really foul things to one another. During one of these arguments, I called out to the Lord, and He said to me, "Heather, that hurts."

Hurts? How does it hurt you?! You are not even a part of this Jesus! This is all my husbands fault! Not yours!

Then, He whispered to my spirit:

"And the King will say, 'I tell you the truth, when you did it to one of the least of these my brothers and sisters, you were doing it to me!'"—Matthew 24:40

In the midst of that fight, I was not only hurting myself and my husband, but I was hurting the Lord. The One who died for my sins; the One who chose me; the One who walks with me; the One who pours wisdom into me daily. Instead of getting mad at the devil and the spirit of division, I was making this a physical fight and not a spiritual one.

And, then I heard this:

"Love is patient and kind. Love is not jealous or boastful or proud or rude. It does not demand its own way. It is not irritable, and it keeps no record of being wronged. It does not rejoice about injustice but rejoices whenever the truth wins out. Love never gives up, never loses faith, is always hopeful, and endures through every circumstance."— 1 Corinthians 13:4-7

Love keeps no record of being wronged and as bad as I wanted to "charge" Cornelius, I desperately needed the same grace from the Lord.

I'm not sure what you've been through in your marriage—whether it's infidelity, deceit, or you simply feel like you no longer love your spouse. I know the situation may be hard to bare, but I have found that everything I need for the perfect will of God for my life is found under my last name. The covenant of marriage is where I will find my healing if I don't leave it. If I stay in my marriage and I refuse to run from it, the Lord will continue to reveal who I really am through my marriage.

You see, marriage exposes your weaknesses, your strengths, your attitude and your heart. Too often we run away from our spouse when things get tough and we don't go through the process. There is a reason that the bible says to rejoice in hard times!

"Even though I have received such wonderful revelations from God. So to keep me from becoming proud, I was given a thorn in my flesh, a messenger from Satan to torment me and keep me from becoming proud. Three different times I begged the Lord to take it away. Each time he said, 'My grace is all you need. My power works best in weakness.' So now I am glad to boast about my weaknesses, so that the power of Christ can work through me. That's why I take pleasure in my weaknesses, and in the insults, hardships, persecutions, and troubles that I suffer for Christ. For when I am weak, then I am strong."—2 Corinthians 12:7-10

I have learned that with every peak and every valley, I learn something new in my marriage and about myself.

Early on in our marriage, I was very controlling. When my husband wanted to get a haircut or go to the gym without me, I would feel rejected. Once we had a discussion about why this was such an issue for me, we discovered fear as the root. My fear was that something bad would happen to my husband. I had watched my mother become a widow two different times with men that she adored. I walked with her during those seasons and I continue to walk with her. I found that I took on the fear of, "What if?" "What if something happened and I wasn't there? What if I'm a widow! What if?"

The Lord showed my husband that I was dealing with fear, rejection and abandonment and the Lord used my marriage to heal me. I began to identify my fears and struggles and I took those things to the Lord and laid them at His feet. Before I was married, I justified my struggles and accepted them as a part of my life but after being married, I thank God that my husband washed me with the water of the Word (Ephesians 5) and showed me this area that I struggled with for years. *He was a mirror to me so I could no longer hide behind excuses.* So now I am thankful for those rough moments and seasons. I do believe that you have to get through those rough times to see what is on the other side of trusting the Lord. If you don't feel like devoting energy to changing your marriage, I have good news.

The good news?

Your feelings can change and God can still raise a dead marriage. I have literally watched the Lord change our entire marriage and make it brand new. Marriage is literally two people that are waking up and saying yes to the Lord everyday. If your spouse isn't saved, it is still you saying yes to God, *even if the love is not reciprocated.* I have had times in my own marriage where I felt like my husband wasn't loving me like Christ loved the church, and I know he has had times where he felt like I wasn't respecting him, but it didn't stop us in that moment from freely loving the other unconditionally. So if you feel like you're the only one loving, caring and trying, hang in there. Keep planting good seeds. God will never fail you.

But Heather, I married the wrong person.

How many times have I thought that I made a mistake in marrying Cornelius? Maybe 40-50 times in our almost seven years of marriage and especially during our first year. I thought, "Oh, God! I wish I would have married someone that was more like this or that," which was a lie because everyone has issues so if it weren't this particular issue, it would be something else.

I can relate to you. I know things are hard. I know you don't understand. I know you want out. I know you've read stories of people who left their marriages and are happy now. I know you're wondering if that could be you. I am telling you this: Refuse to compare your marriage to any other marriage on this earth. There is no marriage that is unique or quite like your marriage. There's no husband or no wife like the covenant you both have created together. Compare your life to Jesus only and ask the Holy Spirit what you should do. If you're too busy and too cluttered, you will never hear from the Lord and the voices of many will send you to divorce court. Protect your marriage. Connect with a couple that will hold you accountable while pushing you towards the Word. Most of all, spend tons of time with Jesus and stay on your face until He shows you what to do.

God healed my dead marriage. It's still not perfect, but we are striving for perfection daily. He can do the same for you.

Oh, how prideful and blind I was during this season! I have a really good friend whose husband dealt with pornography and adultery. She had every reason to leave him because she was rightfully mad and upset, but instead she stayed in her marriage. They sought counseling together and recognized the areas they had opened doors for the enemy. Now they have a beautiful family and their marriage is thriving. I recall him getting off of social media for a season because it was a stronghold for him. I saw him attending church with his family instead of working every Sunday. I saw them go to counseling individually and together. They created a plan and decided to fight for their marriage.

The story of Mary and Joseph dropped into my spirit as I was preparing for this chapter.

"This is how the birth of Jesus the Messiah came about: His mother Mary was pledged to be married to Joseph, but before they came together, she was found to be pregnant through the Holy Spirit. Because Joseph her husband was faithful to the law, and yet did

*not want to expose her to public disgrace, he
had in mind to divorce her quietly.*

*But after he had considered this, an angel of
the Lord appeared to him in a dream and
said, 'Joseph son of David, do not be afraid to
take Mary home as your wife, because what
is conceived in her is from the Holy Spirit. She
will give birth to a son, and you are to give
him the name Jesus, because he will save his
people from their sins.'*

*All this took place to fulfill what the Lord said
through the prophet: 'The virgin will conceive
and give birth to a son, and they will call him
Immanuel (Which means God with us).'*

*When Joseph woke up, he did what the angel
of the Lord had commanded him and took
Mary home as his wife. But he did not
consummate their marriage until she gave
birth to a son. And he gave him the name
Jesus."—Matthew 1:19-25*

We must recognize that Mary was young, poor, and
a woman; which during that time, meant she was
considered unusable by God for any major task, but God
used her for one of the most important acts of obedience.
Joseph had every right to leave Mary when she became
pregnant without them ever consummating their

marriage. It appeared as if she had been unfaithful and based on Jewish Civil Law he could have had Mary stoned to death. In his own understanding, Joseph was doing the "right" thing based on the law of the land, but when the Lord told him to stay there, regardless of what it looked like, Joseph had to trust Him.

So, what is your marriage facing? Yes, it may appear that you are very justified in leaving but, if you could ask the Holy Spirit to soften your heart and to show you the way, *He may be encouraging you to work out your marriage after that adultery.* I know everyone around you is telling you to leave but if you sense the Holy Spirit saying that He has a plan for your marriage, even in the midst of the mess, you may find ministry birthed there. Don't run just because it *looks* really bad. Instead, seek the Lord. And consider no one else's opinion. The Lord is capable of healing your marriage.

Chapter 6

Fighting for Intimacy

Most couples assume that intimacy in a marriage is all about sex, but that's not all there is to it. While sex is an important part of marriage, it's not the only thing that defines the intimacy in your relationship. There isn't much sex when stress, frustration, financial problems, and countless other distractions are present in your marriage. Defining the key spiritual components of intimacy will help to sustain you when encountering difficulties in your marriage.

Plainly put, intimacy is closeness. It is where someone or something is allowed to go "in-to-me-to-see" what others cannot. Intimate friendships are those where you have a deeper connection and closeness that everyone else doesn't have. They know things about you that others don't. They are allowed to see things that others cannot see. This closeness is created by experiences and based entirely on trust. Very few can journey that road and have access to parts of you that others aren't entitled to.

This type of connection is mandatory for marriage. The two of you are able to explore the depths of each other's hearts in a way that others cannot. You're able to dive deep beyond the shallow ends of the ocean and truly see what is hidden within your partner's heart. Over time, a spouse may uncover things she or he didn't expect. You may say, "Well, we lived together before we got married and we've known each other for years." That's great and all, but that doesn't mean you've been able to journey below the surface and truly see what's hidden underneath. Living together allows for you to see certain preferences like what time the person wakes up, how they like their coffee, how they like the kitchen cleaned, etc., but it doesn't mean the two of you are truly intimate. I've sat with couples that have been together for years, but they feel like they're just roommates. This is because they've shared a bed, they've shared their bodies, but they've never shared their hearts. Their house is intertwined, their money is intertwined, but their hearts are far from one another. There's an old O' Jay's song I grew up hearing over and over again at my great grandmother's home that went: "Your body's here with me, but your mind is on the other side of town." These words are true for many marriages today. While they live together, they don't truly know each other.

Intimacy is a deeper level of knowing. It is possible for you to know about someone, without actually knowing their character or deepest truths. You know *of* the public figures you follow on social media, but you haven't spent time with them to really *know* them personally. Truly knowing your spouse is important and comes only from spending the quality time that brings about their personal truths.

Adultery can be the result of a spouse finding more comfort in truly knowing someone outside of their home. This is where he or she begins to confide in the secretary, co-worker, housekeeper, or boss. The spouse spends more time intimately sharing his or her heart with someone who doesn't deserve to know that side of them. That's an act of treason against the marriage and is considered adultery even before a sexual act occurs. Most believe that the act of adultery begins when two people share their bodies with one another but that's usually the last stop on the journey of infidelity. Before getting there they have already consummated an illegal covenant through intimate conversation. They've revealed to an outsider some things that should have only been discussed between the confines of their home.

Matthew 5:27-28 reads, "You heard it was said, 'Do not commit adultery,' but I say to you that everyone who looks at a woman in order to covet her has already committed adultery with her in his heart." Many believe that Jesus was "intensifying" the Law with what He said, but that's not necessarily true. The Tenth Commandment says, "Thou shalt not covet." This is in reference to coveting another person's spouse, house, yard, car, pets, or anything else owned by your neighbor. Jesus' words seek to let us know that the Law prohibits adultery and coveting. They are both equally dangerous, and sinful, but Jesus isn't referring to the desire itself because we know that to be tempted is not a sin. The sin is when we give in to the temptation that seeks to overtake us. Jesus is not condemning those who are tempted. The desire can exist, but it becomes wrong when what's desired breeds action or becomes an idol, therefore distracting us from what God has for us, or what he has already given us.

King David looked on Bathsheba. The temptation was present when he looked at her; however, the sin didn't happen until the desire manifested into a request.

> *"Late one afternoon, after his mid day rest, David got out of bed and was walking on the roof of the palace. As he looked out over the city, he noticed a woman of unusual beauty taking a bath. He sent someone to find out who she was, and he was told, 'She is Bathsheba, the daughter of Eliam and the wife of Uriah the Hittite.' Then David sent messengers to get her; and when she came to the palace, he slept with her."*— *2 Samuel 11:2-4*

Notice that David was tempted, but he yielded to it. He sent for her—the physical act (sin) of what he desired.

Fighting for Intimacy

Intimacy is the sharing of hearts:

*"You brood of snakes! How could evil men
like you speak what is good and right? For
whatever is in your heart determines what
you say."*

It's true to say that out of the abundance of the heart, the mouth speaks. The heart overflows whatever is in it, and we're able to speak to one another based on whatever comes out of our heart. This is important because whomever you communicate with has the potential to obtain what's in your heart. Communication is the bridge that connects two hearts together. If one bridge collapses, the connection ceases to exist. This makes it easy for a husband and wife to live in the same home but never truly know each other. They casually communicate but it isn't heartfelt.

Because intimacy is the closeness between two people it should be a mandatory aspect of any marriage. You and your spouse should seek being close with one another as much as possible. Sharing your heart with one another intensifies the love between you and decreases the chances of looking else where to confide, and ultimately divorce. It decreases the chances because you share everything with each other. It's difficult to hide things from someone who really knows you.

Intimacy also intensifies the sexual encounter between you and your spouse. It's one thing to stimulate a person's body, but it's something totally different to stimulate their mind before ever touching them. Sex begins when the two intertwine as one, but intimacy precedes it. It can also determine the experience. There should be spiritual substance. Sex between a married couple should never be reduced only to what the two physically get out of it, but what they are building by coming together in such an intimate way. Sex in marriage should be exciting and fun, and what makes it so exciting and fun is the intimacy between you and your husband. You know each other so deeply that you enjoy making each other happy. You enjoy serving one another and you prefer each other. In fact, you work hard to make sure your spouse's sexual experience is the best ever! You seek to satisfy instead of being satisfied.

My wife and I know personally what it's like to have things that happen in life distract you from being intimate with one another. There are times when we're not home for most of the month and it isn't easy traveling from hotel to hotel, rental car to rental car, event to event. And, don't even mention the fact that we co-sleep with our two children. Through all of these things we have to make time for each other. Notice I did not say that we had to *find* time for one another. Finding time implies that it might not be available. I can seek to find something and not get what I'm looking for—instead, we make time. That means we take certain things off our schedule to make sure we have that special time together. We schedule a date day every Friday, family day is every Saturday and we take at least one trip together a year. We also find events and attractions to do alone to enjoy time with each other. These things are important to us. They help us with our communication, which deepens our intimacy.

You keep intimacy in your home and marriage by constantly communicating with one another, keeping others out of your intimate conversations, and preferring one another over and over again. Consider the words you've read and realize that your marriage is worth fighting for. The intimacy in your home is worth fighting for. And you and your spouse are worth fighting for. I know what it's like to not like to talk, but marriage is about being selfless. A spouse cannot expect to give him or herself to the world while feeding their spouse scraps. Your spouse deserves every bit of you. And if there are some things that bother you about each other, converse about them. Don't grow silent. Silent rage is the invisible monster that separates close friends. If losing weight is important to you, explain it to your spouse. Workout together. Don't allow anyone or anything to destroy the intimacy in your home. Fight together!

Chapter 7

Who Does What?

I can recall travelling to preach at a particular men's conference that was absolutely amazing. The presence of God was so thick in that room and I witnessed men being healed from their emotional wounds. After I preached, we worshipped the Lord for almost two hours. Men wept and travailed. Many just sat in their seats in awe of what was taking place. Afterwards, I started fighting against the thoughts that I had anything to do with what took place in that church. Men kept walking up to me to tell me how much they appreciated me. I was fighting against allowing the compliments to go to my head. I was on a spiritual high.

That night, I went back to my hotel and caught the first flight home as I do for most of my solo speaking engagements. I replayed everything that happened that night over and over in my mind for the entire plane ride, and I was still on a spiritual high as I drove home from the airport. When I arrived home, my wife greeted me with a hug and kiss, handed me our son, and told me that the trash was overflowing and one of the toilets was backed up again. *It was in that moment that I got a heavy dose of reality and humility. It doesn't matter what you do or who you think you are, there are always chores to be done.*

One of the major issues that creates a great deal of frustration and anger in the household is who is responsible for doing what. Titus 2:3-5 explains that a woman is the keeper of the home. This means she is to guard her dwelling place. She is to be fully aware of the activities, structure, tone, and routine in the home. She takes the responsibility of maintaining peace, and makes sure that her family's dwelling is more than a house, but a comfort. She makes it so peaceful that her family considers home the place they're able to vacate from the stresses and pressures of the world. Unfortunately, our society has moved far away from this reality. We teach our young women to be greater successes outside of the home than within them. We also do a greater disservice by not teaching the young men the honor, pleasure, and duty of helping in the home.

I grew up in a house where my mother did everything. My mom and dad are still married to this day and he has always been present in my life, but he wasn't active. This forced my mother to care for the home and take on many of the responsibilities that should have been shared with my father. Although it is biblically sound for a woman to keep the home, it is foolish for a man to think she should have to do it alone. It is wrong for a man to think that she should care for their children alone. A mother and wife is never called to shoulder the responsibility of the home and the children while the man focuses only on work and other extracurricular activities. In fact, it is biblically sound for the father to teach his children the Scriptures. It is his responsibility to instruct them in godliness and train them in a way of righteousness so they don't depart from it when they're older. The duties of the father and husband of a home doesn't end at bringing home money and throwing it at his family. It doesn't stop at saying he provided a roof over their head and food on the table. It doesn't stop at buying them all the things he felt his family wanted. His responsibility continues as he governs the home that his wife keeps, making sure it is properly kept with his faithful assistance, godly leadership, and Spirit-led direction.

I watched my mother work very hard in our home. She would often make very large meals and many of our family would come over to eat. She would cook the food, wash the dishes, and put everything away. She did this until my sister and I were old enough to do it ourselves. I was a chubby kid that absolutely loved food, and I loved to be independent. I didn't like waiting on anyone to do things for me, so I started scrambling my own eggs when I was about 3-years-old. I'd push a chair to the stove, crack the eggs, and stir them around until they were done cooking. My mother would cultivate my cooking by teaching me several of her methods. This carried out of the kitchen as I learned how to properly do laundry, sweep floors, and I shared the duties of washing the dishes with my sister.

One would think that my chores stopped there, but I was still told to go outside and mow the lawn, take out the trash, clean the garage, and rake the leaves. My father would sometimes take me outside with him to watch as he changed the oil or fixed a flat tire. My upbringing was definitely well-rounded, and I was especially thankful for it after I moved out of my parent's home for the second time. There I was in a home by myself and I knew how to do my own laundry, cook my own food, and clean my own home. I wasn't dependent on anyone to do anything. What I loved about it was that I didn't feel as if I needed a wife to come complete me; instead, I would ask God for a wife to compliment me. Only Christ can complete you, but a spouse can compliment you. She or he adds to you, or they can also subtract.

Heather did most of the cooking and cleaning when we first got married. She worked from home, so it was easy for her to do things in the house while I was away working in my office. I walked into a home with a warm meal, a bath, and the smell of a nice fragrance. It was wonderful! However, that started to change the busier she became. She went from having no one but me around to overseeing an international women's ministry and our children. Her responsibilities really picked up, but one thing I really respect about my wife is that *she never allowed those things to conflict with her duties at home.*

Who Does What?

I can admit that I can be a bit messy. I can come home from church and throw my suit on top of the hangers that are sitting on the bed, or throwing my dirty clothes next to the hamper instead of putting them inside. It's those little things that can cause major irritations so when I noticed that she was becoming overwhelmed with the responsibility, I took her out to dinner so we could talk about how I could make things easier for her. I offered to help around the house here and there: I cooked my own breakfast, washed a couple loads of clothes, and took the dishes out of the dishwasher instead of just waiting on Heather to do it. I stepped in wherever we felt it was most appropriate. Instead of my wife feeling like she had to cook a different meal for breakfast, lunch, and dinner, I asked if she could make a big meal that I could eat multiple times a day or for multiple days. This helped her to use her time wisely so she could be free to do other things that needed to be done.

As both of our responsibilities continued to increase, something more needed to be done. I didn't want to compromise the work in the home for what we were seeking to do outside of it, so I asked my wife if we could bring someone in to deep clean our home every two weeks. Maximizing our time meant bringing in someone to fulfill menial duties and tasks around the house that would otherwise be forgotten as we needed to devote our time to other important areas.

You might read that and say, "But I can't afford to hire help!" There was a time when we couldn't either. In fact, it's not a perfectly ideal situation for us even now. I viewed assisting my wife with the chores around the house two ways; either I can do it or I can pay someone to do it. To me, my time is more important than my money, so I sacrificed other things I'd normally buy eating out so I could afford someone to assist us around the house. You might say, "Well, that's great, but we still don't have money to do that either!" That's fine. As a husband, I have a responsibility of providing for my household, which is based on 1 Timothy 5:8. I cannot expect my wife to keep a home that we do not have. I also have a biblical responsibility of being active in the area of disciplining and rearing our children (1 Timothy 3:3-5; Colossians 3:21).

As men, we should not think that our job is to provide the living arrangements and food while the wife and mother handles the children and home duties alone. As an act of love, we should desire to assist one another wherever there is a need. For one to see their spouse in need and not help is wrong. Some things are very simple like picking up behind yourself. Like Christ does with the Church, desire to make the way easy for your partner. That means you need to go the extra mile to make sure you help wherever you are needed. That is how a husband loves his wife, and it is how a wife submits herself to her husband as unto Christ.

Both husband and wife must see the value in sharing a commitment to the success of the home. It is important that expectations are communicated and managed, while coming to a compromise so that both are satisfied with how things are completed. I can recall a time where Heather and I got into a nasty argument over a pile of clothes in our closet. While I was at work, I was bothered enough about the clutter to ask my wife to clean it before I got home. She told me she had a break in her day, and I assumed we agreed that she would use that time to straighten our closet. Well when I got home from work and the clutter was still there, I became angry and an argument followed that resulted in both of us saying hurtful things and a thick tension in our home. Once we came together to discuss where we went wrong, Heather was upset that I didn't notice how clean the rest of the house was because I was only focused on the unkempt closet. I failed to see that the floors were swept, the tables were wiped down, the dishes were clean, and a hot meal was on the kitchen table for me when I arrived home. I didn't see what she had done because I was only focused on what I felt like she didn't do. I was focused on the clutter while she was focused on the rest of our home.

Both of us had an idea of what we expected to be clean. I was frustrated because my expectations were not met, and it showed us that our preferences are not the same. This moment brought clarity that manifests in other areas of our married life: Heather focuses on the bigger picture, while I take pride in the small details. The focus of this is to make sure you and your spouse are clear on the expectations when it comes to who does what in the home. While the small details may be important to you, those same things might not be as important to your spouse. Having an open and honest discussion about this helps to ease future frustrations.

Effective communication is the solution for a multitude of problems. Reference the Word of God as it pertains to the duties of the home, which places wives and mothers as keepers of the home and husbands and fathers as priests and overseers. We held off from listing certain responsibilities *because only you and your spouse can decide what works best for you.* My wife and I have a very traditional view—one in which we believe is in line with the Word of God and works for us. Having these traditional roles allows us to practice our faith in the manner that we choose. It allows for the Word of God to dictate our household instead of us dictating it ourselves. It is also important to note that we discussed these roles and responsibilities early on in our courtship. We were both very direct in our questioning and sharing of our expectations with one another, as well as going to the Lord in prayer about them.

One thing that really helped us was how we chose to see the duties in our home. A lot of times married couples will seek to split their responsibilities down the middle, instead of being all in for whatever needs to be done at that particular time. *Marriage is meant to be a full commitment, not a halfway effort.* It isn't a swim in the shallow end of the ocean; it is a full dive in the deep with your spouse. It is where the two of you are fully immersed together. It is the giving of 100% of each other to one another. Heather and I have met couples who stopped at giving just 50% of themselves to their spouse and to the work in the home. They developed a 'keeping score' mentality that would ultimately backfire on them. This made it easy for one spouse to hold the other in contempt for not doing what they originally committed to.

While that's a great way to run a military camp, it doesn't really work well for marriage. Marriage is meant to be a healthy mixture of unconditional love, grace, and mercy. These three ingredients are paramount in the health and viability of any union. There's very little grace and mercy found in holding your spouse in contempt for failing to wash the dishes the night before. While it might be annoying, it isn't the end of the world. It could have been that they were tired or that they had a lot on their mind. *Too often we run quickly to the charge without considering the reason.* If you have truly laid down your life for your spouse, which is the ultimate act of love, then you'd consider sharing those responsibilities with your spouse. This means you'd wash the dishes instead of complaining about how your spouse failed to do it. Believe it or not, you aren't above the chores that you think are biblically assigned to your spouse. Remember that the goal is to get the chores done, not how they get done— even if it's you who has to do them.

Don't get me wrong, my wife and I have certain responsibilities that we prefer over others, but we aren't afraid to jump in and help where needed. My wife has taken out the trash, and I have washed the dishes.

Fighting Together

There was one time when I got home from work to find the kitchen a big mess. My wife makes great food, but she is a messy cook. She uses every pan, measuring cup, spoon, fork, and knife in the kitchen and she's just making pancakes (Hey, I use a lot of ingredients. ☺ *HL edit)! I walked into the house, and the sink was piled with dishes. I immediately called for Heather but got no response. I was fuming! When I went upstairs, she was laid across the bed asleep. I immediately woke her up because I wanted to know why the kitchen was so dirty. The dishes were supposed to be her responsibility. I could tell that she was tired, but I didn't care because I felt tired too. She got up and listened to me go on and on about what wasn't done, until eventually she got up and told me that I was ungrateful.

I couldn't understand how she was flipping this on me as if I did something wrong. It wasn't until a couple days later that I realized the error of my ways. I walked in the house and threw my things down at the door instead of organizing them like I should have. I didn't hold myself accountable to that, in the same way I was trying to hold Heather accountable to the dishes. I focused on the dirty dishes in the sink, but I failed to see the freshly cooked meal waiting for me on the stove with a sweet note on it from my wife. *The note was about how much she loved being my wife and how tired she was because of her job. I passed the note to go confront my wife instead of going to console her.* I was so upset about what wasn't done that I didn't think to consider what she actually did, especially since what she did outweighed what I felt wasn't done.

While in prayer later that week I brought this up to God. I wanted so bad to be justified in my anger towards Heather even though I knew I was wrong. While venting my frustration I believe He impressed upon my heart these words: *"Dishes aren't gender specific!"* I almost flat lined in that moment. Those words stung straight to my heart. It was from that day forward that my perspective changed, and I challenged myself to mature in that area. Instead of becoming frustrated at what I think wasn't done, I needed to be thankful for what was and jump in to help wherever I was needed.

Here's the challenge to myself: if I'm so upset about what isn't done then I should probably roll up my sleeves and do it myself. Getting angry at my wife isn't going to help the situation. I've found myself jumping in to do the dishes or mopping the floor many times, and my wife would come up to me and thank me for understanding. *While we do have help in our home with our children, they constantly follow my wife around all day.* She is a very productive woman who's tasked to juggle many things. It's not always feasible for her to spend countless hours in the kitchen or washing clothes. She sees those things as her responsibilities, but we know that effective companionship means we must work together. The same goes for you in your household. Yes, chores need to be done, but they shouldn't cause tension between you and your spouse. Effectively communicate your expectations, be graceful and merciful, recruit help from paid contractors to assist in the home, prefer one another, and work together. Prayerfully this healthy mixture will steer you and your spouse in the right direction.

Chapter 8

Finances

I heard for years before getting married that finances were one of the main reasons that marriages end in divorce. I never understood until we were married and hit in this area.

If you don't have a healthy relationship with money and understand your purpose as a married couple, it can easily become an idol between the two of you. Many people work excessively to "provide" or to acquire material possessions they never had as children only to neglect God, our ultimate provider.

The first time the Bible mentions someone wealthy; it speaks of a righteous man, Abraham, who, *"was very rich in livestock, in silver, and in gold"* (Genesis 13:2). Later, we find God promising that through this man's descendants, all nations of the earth would be blessed (Genesis 18:18; Genesis 22:18; Genesis 26:4.) Abraham was wealthy, but he was also "the father of all those who believe (Romans 4:11)." This is the first of many examples that God is not opposed to riches; in fact, He is the originator of financial blessings (1 Samuel 2:7; Proverbs 10:22) and reminds us that personal diligence can also lead to wealth (Proverbs 10:4).

When we have more money than we need for normal expenses, we are to be wise to save for later use and be advised through Holy Spirit and physical facts on where to invest what the Lord has given us. The Bible speaks highly of the saver, noting that the ant wisely stores up food for the winter (Proverbs 6:6-11). It speaks favorably of someone who would provide for his children and grandchildren:

> *"A good man leaves an inheritance to his*
> *children's children, but the wealth of the*
> *sinner is stored up for the righteous."—*
> *Proverbs 13:22*

As written, it is biblical to provide for your children and grandchildren in and out of this life on earth. If you haven't already, invest in life insurance to leave your family with *something* no matter how old you are! Having more money puts us in a better position to do the will of God for our lives. We definitely went through a season where we couldn't help anyone but even when we didn't have much, we gave as the Holy Spirit instructed. *Money truly proves your heart.* If you are lustful and rebellious to God without money, you will only be lustful and rebellious with money. Money simply amplifies what is in your heart.

As believers, those who want to make money while continuing to follow God must avoid certain spiritual traps. It can become easy to accumulate worldly goods or to look to money for stability rather than God, but He warns us against this (Proverbs 18:11).

The apostle Paul also talked about money and temptation:

> *"Those who desire to be rich fall into temptation and a snare, and into many foolish and harmful lusts which drown men in destruction and perdition. For the love of money is a root of all kinds of evil, for which some have strayed from the faith in their greediness, and pierced themselves through with many sorrows."—1 Timothy 6:9-10*

It is from these words that many get the idea that the Bible teaches that *money* is the root of all evil; however, Paul wrote something considerably different — that "the *love of money* is a root of all kinds of evil." Money by itself *is not evil*, but being consumed with the idea of money, chasing after the accumulation of it at all costs, and pursuing money and material wealth by making it a bigger priority to you than pursuing Christ, is the true evil. In this passage Paul discusses the perspective toward wealth that Jesus gave many years earlier. In looking at a Christian's proper priorities (Matthew 6:24-33), Jesus said, *"You cannot serve God and mammon"* (Matthew 6:24). The English *mammon* is translated here from a similar Aramaic word that means "riches." God explicitly tells us that you can not be fully committed to Him and simultaneously consumed with pursuing wealth, and that in choosing it as an idol you abandon the Father. In that sense, wealth is personified as a competing master, which is unacceptable.

Jesus understands that you have physical needs but He emphasized that our chief priority must always be God. Jesus taught, "Seek first the kingdom of God and His righteousness, and all these things shall be added to you (Matthew 6:33)." I love how Paul teaches us to not make a god of money or to allow it to come before God, but I am reiterating that we should not allow for it to come between our relationship with God *or* with our spouse. Money is simply a tool that can be used for good or bad, and our perspective and attitude towards it will determine our mindset.

If the position of our heart is good and we are responsible stewards over what God has given us, we can truly learn to be faithful with more.

What Works for Your Marriage?

We learned early on in our marriage that I was just a tad bit better with managing our finances. The beautiful thing about marriage is that if one person is stronger in the area of organizing and budgeting, then it is the complete trust of your partner that allows you to relinquish control and allow that spouse to handle the money. It's important that you figure out what works for *your* marriage.

When we first got married we had one money pot. Why? Because we were broke and we didn't have a whole lot. As we learned to budget and save, we found that one main account for bills with two separate personal accounts, works for us. This allows for us to surprise each other with things as we desire. We also have personal savings, investments, and retirement accounts. Even though I manage most of these accounts, my husband still oversees the process and there are no "secret" accounts. Both of our names are on everything, because together we are one flesh.

If you and your spouse have separate viewpoints on who should manage the money, look to the Word for guidance, but first pray. If your finances are completely out of order, it's time to get the Lord back at the center of it all.

"If there is famine in the land, if there is pestilence or blight or mildew or locust or caterpillar, if their enemies besiege them in the land at their gates, whatever plague, whatever sickness there is, whatever prayer,

*whatever plea is made by any man or by all
your people Israel, each knowing his own
affliction and his own sorrow and stretching
out his hands toward this house, then hear
from heaven your dwelling place and forgive
and render to each whose heart you know,
according to all his ways, for you, you only,
know the hearts of the children of
mankind."—2 Chronicles 6:28-30*

I cannot stress this enough, pray before you move forward. Pray for a patient spirit with your spouse, for a content heart, and for honesty. If you have a wrong relationship with money, now is the time to talk it out honestly. If you fear not having money and work long hours because you're afraid of lacking, then this is the time to air it out.

Bring it all together.

Luke 16:11 asks, "If then you have not been faithful in the unrighteous wealth, who will entrust to you the true riches?"

It's time to get your finances in order! Do you know how much debt you have together? Gather your checkbooks, bank statements, and insurance documents in one place. Make sure that you include your joint accounts and discuss the amount of debt you have with the perspective interest rates. We like to maintain an excel spreadsheet with our exact debt and goals for when things will be paid off. It's tough to total up that number and realize that you never need to shop again—well, at least for a season! Don't forget to budget and pull money aside for staycations, conferences and marriage retreats. These things will help your marriage and it's vital that you make time to pull away from the norm.

After you total up your debt, write up your assets. What are your cars worth based on the current bluebook value? How much do you have in savings or investments?

Consider what you have.

Matthew 25:14-30 – remember the parable of the master who left his money in the charge of three different servants?

> *"For to everyone who has will more be given,*
> *and he will have an abundance. But from the*
> *one who has not, even what he has will be*
> *taken away."—Matthew 25:29*

Do you both have life insurance policies? Can you understand the statements on your investments? Have you pulled your credit card report to see if everything is accurate? How much are you paying in interest on your current loans? Does your cash flow well or do all of your bills seem to be due on one day of the month? Did you know that you could even dispute things that are on your credit report? It's true that bad marks are removed after 7 years but you don't have to wait 7 years if the bill has been settled.

Be diligent and intentional in managing what you do have, before desiring more. We will have to give an account of what God entrusted us with, so be sure that you are proactive about what you have been given.

Agree on a plan.

Maybe you can only agree to put all receipts and bills next to the computer this week. This might be the month you agree to a budget by making a plan for how to spend your money before it arrives in your account. This could be the time to schedule an appointment with a financial representative to understand those mutual funds or research life insurance prices. Whether you can agree on a plan for the next 48 hours or the next 48 months, determine what your next steps are before you end the discussion on finances.

These steps may be harder than anything you've faced as a couple. You may experience a wide range of feelings, but they will not change the truth. The truth about your current financial standing or the truth about what God can do through your marriage as you seek His

Finances

Word for wisdom in managing it. When we manage our resources well, we can meet the needs of those God puts in our lives. This stretching that you're experiencing is for your good. Let the Lord prune you and show you your heart.

As I mentioned in the beginning, finances are one of the major reasons for divorce and in the name of Jesus, you will not let a piece of paper come in between you and your spouse!

Chapter 9

The In-Laws, Extended Family, and Friends

There should be a sign created for married couples that tells in-laws, extended family, and friends to refrain from diving into your marital affairs unless asked. Too bad no such sign exists that most would follow!

We have dealt with the drama that comes from in-laws, extended family, and friends more times than we can count and it is a reoccurring issue discussed in many of our marriage counseling sessions. While there have been many issues, we shouldn't discount the importance and value of having family around.

Humans are relational people; therefore, relationships are important to us. They help us grow and create an environment of encouragement and assistance in our difficult moments. They are there to help and to be a supportive community. They hold us accountable; pick us up when we're broken, and commune with us when we're lonely. Having a great support system is vital to the sustainability of any person and family. Believe it or not, family and friends serve a valuable purpose in your marriage. We often hear how outside opinions from family and friends can ruin a relationship, but they can really help and support a godly marriage.

Family provides encouragement. We all need encouragement, and your marriage will need a lot of it. Their encouragement should always be Christ-centered and founded in love. You will know when what they are telling you isn't worth listening to when their words are opposite the Word of God. For example, you should not listen to the aunt who constantly tells you to get a divorce just because your spouse doesn't do everything right; instead, you should listen to the cousin who is urging you to forgive and become more selfless. They encourage both of you to live righteously and fight together, never against one another.

Family provides wisdom. I love sitting amongst older generations to hear stories about things they went through in their lives. It allows me to see their perspective and pitfalls so I can grow and avoid the dangers that they went through. It's wise for you and your spouse to listen to godly wisdom from your family. As with encouragement from your family, seek confirmation of the Holy Spirit and look to the scriptures for evidence of what is being said.

The In-Laws, Extended Family, and Friends

Wise counselors also play a key role in the encouragement and accountability of your marriage. Heather and I have couples we know and mutually respect that we allow to speak into our marriage. We expect wise counsel from them, and we are rarely disappointed.

Although embracing the wisdom, encouragement, and wise counsel of friends and family is what helps to build up your community, it is also wise to have proper boundaries as well. You cannot spend your days trying to please them while ignoring the wishes and expectations in your home. Many situations call for your in-laws to actually live with you and your spouse. There may be financial constraints that restrict certain couples from having their own home, maybe you need help with your children, or maybe a parent is ill. We should be thankful we have family we can rely on in those difficult times; still, it is dangerous for a married couple to allow their in-laws to interfere with their marriage or disrupt the peace in their home.

Heather started an online boutique after about a year of us being married. The business boomed very early, and my mother in-love (which is how we refer to our in-laws) offered to help alleviate the burden of Heather hand-making every order by herself. This arrangement worked well until they began to have differences in opinion on how the product should be made. They began to argue more often and the tension began to cause stress for my wife, which was making her upset and frustrated at home. Eventually it got so bad, that I stepped in to make it clear to my mother-in-love that our home would be protected from unnecessary stress at all costs and that we would have to find new help for Heather's business. Heather and I were both nervous that this hiccup would interfere with our trips to visit her family, but I assured her that all would be well. I made sure to greet her mother with love and told her how much I loved and appreciated her despite our misunderstanding. Fortunately, she reciprocated that affection and we were able to move on. My goal wasn't to ruin my relationship with my in-loves. I love them with everything in me, but I wanted to make it clear that my wife is my top priority. I will always take her side no matter the situation.

When dealing with in-laws, friends, and extended family it's important to consider these three things: (1) stand beside your spouse at all times; (2) get out of any toxic environment; (3) don't take everything personal.

You always want to show a sign of unity and togetherness by standing by your spouse no matter what. Your family and friends should know they cannot separate you from them. They should also know that you will not allow for them to demean or belittle your spouse in your presence even if it is in a joking manner. There must be zero tolerance for that kind of behavior. Be very direct in telling your in-laws that they cannot influence your home with bad talk about your marriage or your spouse. No person outside of your home should have so much influence that they have the power to impact what goes on within it. What's important is to show that no one or nothing could interfere in your marriage. No spouse should have to feel inferior around their in-laws. They shouldn't have to feel second behind anyone and they should be affirmed that they come first at all times. In marriage, a husband and wife should always prefer one another over anyone else.

As a married couple, you should avoid any toxic environment that causes friction, animosity, or disruption in your household. There should be proper boundaries in place that prohibit in-laws, friends, or extended family from interfering with the peace in your home or communication between you and your spouse. There should never be a time where your family's words outweigh what you and your spouse have already established. It's also very wise to avoid toxic conversations that demean and disrespect your spouse and your marriage. Some will try to convince you that their intentions are good, but it still isn't worth entertaining. Anyone that comes to be a wedge in your marriage is sent from the enemy. Guard your house and your marriage.

Finally, stop taking everything so personal. It's easy to assume that everyone is out to get you but that isn't always the case. You have to remember that your in-laws, extended family, and friends are just people, and they are entitled to their opinions. Their opinions are not truth, and they do not define you or your marriage. After having our son, family members suggested for us to feed him meat but my wife feels very strongly about allowing our children to make those decisions for themselves when they are of age. The suggestion ultimately upset my wife when the advice became adamant and disrespectful, which caused a major problem with me. I wasn't bothered by the comments because I knew they didn't have ill intentions, but that wasn't the same for my wife. While discussing it later I had to tell her that the mistake she made was in accepting our family member's words as truth. They are entitled to their opinions, but that doesn't mean we have to follow it. The same goes for the both of you. Remain humble enough to listen to wisdom when it's given, but don't ever assume that everything said must be taken as complete truth. Be quick to measure it up to the standard you and your spouse have already established in your home. Take out what is meaningful and leave the rest. They're just opinions, so don't take it so personally.

Keep everything in perspective. Having family and friends is important, but you don't want their involvement to hinder or destroy your marriage. When you and your spouse are put against one another, that's not the time to wage war but the time to fight together. Make the necessary decisions to create proper boundaries, list out expectations, and be willing to respect one another's love for his or her family. Navigating through family and friend drama can be tricky, but God gives us grace and wisdom in how to deal with them through Holy Spirit. Be sober-minded, don't take everything personal, be understanding, forgive quickly, and fight together.

Chapter 10

The Power Couple

The concept of the power couple is commonly glorified amongst our generation as being matched with your ideal mate based on their level of success complimenting yours. This couple is usually attractive according to the world's standards, wealthy, and usually portrays the appearance of having it all together. This image of the world's power couple is very shallow and doesn't encompass what God considers when He designs a mate for you.

When God sent Samuel to anoint one of Jesse's sons as king, Jesse had all of his sons, except one, to stand before him. They all appeared as if they could be the chosen one. Boy after boy had the appearance of a king, but there was only one that was to be chosen. Samuel looked at the first boy, Eliab, and thought the one the Lord had anointed was standing before him; however, in 1 Samuel 16:7 God quickly reminded His prophet of this truth:

Fighting Together

"Do not look at his appearance or at the
height of his stature, because I have rejected
him; for God sees not as man sees, for man
looks at the outward appearance, but the
Lord looks at the heart."

God is not like man. He does not consider the outward appearance and judge solely based on it. He looks deep within a man's heart to judge him and in fact, He would do *without* man's sacrifice if He knows it isn't coming from a pure place. He would rather you take your gift with you from the altar if you still have anger in your heart against your brother or sister. He is very particular at those He calls His own, and He plays no favorites. The world looks at what someone has on, how they speak, what they drive, what they live in, and what kind of job they have to judge their level of power. It would seem like those with the most money or influence are the most powerful, but that is not the case in God's eyes. Since He places so much emphasis on the heart, we should as well! That is the initial place we must begin in analyzing the definition of a true power couple. We must not be infatuated with the world's idea of a power couple, but look to the Word as God defines a truly righteous couple.

The definition is very simple: a couple that finds its hope, desires, and direction in Christ. Jesus is their power that connects, encourages, and upholds the couple. *He is the power*, and they are the couple. Together they become the threefold cord that isn't easily broken. His words govern their life and He alone is the foundation of their home (Matthew 7:24-27). It is all about the Lord and Him alone. This couple walks by faith daily and has an eternity mindset. They refuse to rush ahead of the Lord because they understand that their life is not their own.

With Christ as the power between the two of them, their hearts are changed and renewed. He heals them and leads them down the path of righteousness. He redefines their thinking in regards to sin so they can hate what He hates. He opens the path that leads away from temptation and watches over them. This is the protection over the couple that finds its power in Jesus.

Could you consider for a moment the couple that finds their power and hope in the world? Everything this world has to offer is temporary and dying away as soon as it's born. Even mankind is only alive for a few years before he returns to the dust from which he was made. Anyone who puts his or her hope in this world will be disappointed because it won't last. It's like having your phone connected to a power source that has limited electricity. It will work for a short time, but the power will be cut off soon. The power source looks appealing, but lacks the substance to withstand difficulty. The idea that a couple could be empowered by their fashion sense seems amazing, but what happens when the styles change? It seems great that a couple could be known for their wealth, but what happens when all the money runs out? Nothing of this world can last.

Fighting Together

Many people seek to emulate couples they admire and consider them "goals," until they realize you cannot sustain a marriage on what can be seen or captioned on social media. Unfortunately, if your idea of the perfect marriage is based only on what you can physically see, then most of it is superficial. Please don't think I'm questioning the couple as much as I am the standards. I believe our society sets the bar extremely low for what is deemed "success."

Could we rise to a higher standard and recognize "goals" as a couple that's submitted to Christ? A couple that's focused on the betterment of the community; one that seeks to share eternal truths and live as an example worth emulating; one that honors their marriage vows and remains committed to each other for the rest of their lives; one that is willing to sacrifice themselves for the betterment of other people; one that raises their children together and teaches them the Word of God? Could we rise as a people to see that true goals should be only what is acceptable to the Lord? They should give glory to His name.

I know your marriage won't look like everyone else's, but we should all have goals that we are striving to meet. It is perfectly fine for you to admire other Godly couples as they seek Christ first in their marriage—like the younger Timothy to the older Apostle Paul, follow them as they follow Christ. Just make sure they are truly following God. You will know it by their fruit.

The Power Couple

Finally, a righteous power couple doesn't place the emphasis and importance on themselves. Instead, they seek to empower and inspire others to live righteously. Consider many of the couples you think are power couples today—would you be able to say that they live righteously and encourage others too as well? Are they living for themselves or for the betterment of other people? Are they serving the Lord with their substance? A great place to look for an outward example is your pastor and his wife. If you don't have one, I highly recommend you and your spouse become submitted to one. Honor them by submitting to their authority. They have been given a command from God to watch over your souls. Cherish their words more than the words of the top athletes, singers, and movie stars. Just make sure they are truly following Christ so you and your spouse are able to follow them. Make sure they demonstrate the power of God in their lives. It's that power that will sustain them, and it's that same power that will sustain you and your spouse in your marriage. Be a power couple worth emulating! Be strong in the Lord and the power of His might!

Chapter 11

A Discontented Heart

Have you ever felt like the choices you've made in the past weren't the best? Maybe you feel stuck in a not so happy marriage, stuck with a bunch of screaming children you prayed for or just stuck in a job that you absolutely hate. Regardless of where you are in your life you are not alone.

I was once at a job that I despised while feeling totally purposeless, I was once not content with being childless, and during that first year of my marriage and you better believe that I felt stuck in my marriage and wanted OUT. *I began to evaluate my portions in life and I realized that Heather was the common denominator.* **Me.** I was at the center of my misery for a season when I was single, once I became married, and as I battled discontentment with my purpose. Nothing my husband could do would satisfy me. No amount of vacations, gifts or flowers could fill the frustration in my heart. I wanted so bad to blame everyone and everything around me because I felt like external things could fill the voids in my heart. I cried out to God, *"Lord, if you would just change my husband! If you would just give me a promotion, if I was just this or that, THEN I would be satisfied Lord!"* The Holy Spirit arrested my heart and showed me that a wedding ring didn't change my discontented heart. **The same discontent Heather from my single life had stuck its ugly head into my marriage.** My issue wasn't external, it was internal. There was a war going on in my spirit. As Christians, we must stop going to war with physical means when God has instructed us to fight spiritually! War in prayer! War in fasting! War in guarding your heart! War in renewing your mind!

> *"I rejoiced in the Lord greatly that now at length you have revived your concern for me. You were indeed concerned for me, but you had no opportunity. Not that I am speaking of being in need, for I have learned in whatever situation I am to be content. I know how to be brought low, and I know how to abound. In any and every circumstance, I have learned the secret of facing plenty and hunger, abundance and need. I can do all things through him who strengthens me."—*
> *Philippians 4:10-13*

I needed to learn to be content wherever the Lord placed me. *Just because we live for Jesus doesn't mean that we won't have hard times in our marriage.* Living for Jesus simply means that we have accepted Jesus into our hearts and we live by faith. Getting tested allows for us to share in a tiny bit of the persecution of our Lord Jesus. So guess what? Your marriage is going to get tested. In every circumstance and in every situation, we must learn to trust in the Lord and trust that He can make our hearts content. A spouse, a child, a promotion, or whatever else will not fix that discontentment in your heart. If you aren't careful, you will pass that spirit to your children and the people you come in contact with regularly. Your character can actually corrupt those around you without you even realizing it. (1 Corinthians 15:33)

When things get hard in life, we have a pretty hard time shining the light on our hearts and examining that we could actually be the problem. We begin to look at our bank accounts, our not so present friends, our marital status and what we think we lack. We begin to fantasize what life would be like if we had this or that. We assume that the grass will be greener on the other side if we had that thing that we have begun to idolize. The reality is that the grass is as green as our perspective. When we begin to seek the Lord and see things through the eyes of Christ we will understand that all things are working together for our good (Romans 8:28), that He leads our path (Proverbs 3:5), and that we can capture every crazy thought and make it submit to God's word (2 Corinthians 10:5).

You may feel like you are trying to be content and joyful by serving in church, taking care of your kids, doing your best at work or school, but still you feel like you're constantly last and unappreciated. Maybe you feel like your spouse doesn't tell you that you're pretty, or handsome, or that you're doing a great job, or that you're a great parent. Maybe you feel like you are your biggest fan because everybody else sucks all of your energy and drains you. You prayed for a spouse, you prayed for children, you prayed for this life and now that you have it, it seems like you cannot figure out how to balance everything. Have you ever just thrown up your hands and said, "UGH! THESE PEOPLE ARE DRIVING ME NUTS!" I believe that most people have felt that, "What about me" moment. Why is it that I have to be everything for everyone and I don't get the pat on my back that I "feel like I deserve?"

I think as believers, we have a hard time taking a mirror and putting it up to our faces. We want so bad to be perfect and to be acknowledged for what we do that we don't like to admit that we actually need to change. Maybe it's because we feel like we have so much on our plates, *that fixing ourselves seems like just another burden.* Well you can throw away the to-do list because I'm not here to bash you about your schedule or your priorities and responsibilities. I want to show you your heart. *I want to show you with the Holy Spirit's help that you play a big part in the atmosphere of your home.* You play a big part in the raising of this next generation of children, you play a big part in making your marriage work, and you also have a responsibility in the failure of these things.

A Discontented Heart

You may be thinking, "You don't know my spouse because he or she cheated on me, or did this and that." I hate that they did those things to you. My heart boils as I type these words at what you have had to endure, but in the most loving way, let me ask you a question: Have you done everything in your marriage to make it work? Have you identified your husbands love language and tried to meet his needs? Do you respect, honor and submit to him? **Divorce is not an overnight occurrence.** Divorce is thought out and pursued when you refuse to work on your marriage. Let's take the mirror and look at how we can change without putting the blame on your spouse. I can assure you that if you absolutely give God a chance to work, He will change your heart and your marriage.

My question for you is, what is your motive for doing what you do for your spouse? Do you clean up, are you affectionate, or do you give words of affirmation because you want something in return? Far too often, we try to please our spouses with ourselves in mind. Maybe we have the expectation of having our needs met if we do something we know our spouse likes but this is exactly how the world operates. The world's love is conditional. Instead of focusing on "What About Me?" let's consistently ask, "What About Them?" *How can I best serve my family to bring glory to the Lord?* Remember that how much you truly love Jesus will be demonstrated in how you treat and love your spouse.

I challenge you to deal with what is truly frustrating you. What do you think you need in order to be satisfied? Many times, *God is trying to show us that what we really need is Him.* Intimacy with the Father so that we can remove the clutter and sit quietly before Him for instructions. The beautiful thing about spending time with the Holy Spirit is that He begins to show us ourselves and where we are wrong. For me it was always placing my worth and value in relationships and promotions. I liked to feel important so the Lord had to remove my void-fillers to show me that those things will never satisfy me, and that I must stop blaming everyone and everything for my portion in life.

Here are a few suggestions if you feel like you have a discontented heart:

1. Be intentional about your prayer life and reading your bible uninterrupted. Even if you have to wake up before your family, it's important that you're in tune with the Holy Spirit.

2. Guard your heart. Refuse to watch certain TV shows, read gossip magazines, entertain ungodly conversations, or listen to secular music as all of these things can plant bad seeds in your heart that will harvest discontentment as the fruit.

3. Stir yourself up in the Lord. Refuse to host a pity party and rouse yourself with scripture.

4. Write out your scriptures and put around your house, office, or in a place where you will see them. Meditate on them daily!

5. Get a hobby! Find something that you love to do outside of your responsibilities with home and work, and get busy about serving in your church. Getting your eyes off of yourself and helping someone else helps to put life in perspective!

Chapter 12

HELPMEET

Ladies, this one is for you. Do you know that God has called you to be your husband's helpmeet? What a beautiful honor!

Lets first look at the dictionary definition of a "helpmeet:"

1. a companion and helper.
2. a spouse.
3. anything that aids or assists, especially regularly

Now, lets see what the scripture says:

"The LORD God placed the man in the Garden of Eden to tend and watch over it. But the LORD God warned him, "You may freely eat the fruit of every tree in the garden— except the tree of the knowledge of good and evil. If you eat its fruit, you are sure to die."

Fighting Together

*"Then the LORD God said, 'It is not good for the man to be alone. I will make a **helper** who is just right for him.' So the LORD God formed from the ground all the wild animals and all the birds of the sky. He brought them to the man to see what he would call them, and the man chose a name for each one. He gave names to all the livestock, all the birds of the sky, and all the wild animals. But still there was no helper just right for him.*

So the LORD God caused the man to fall into a deep sleep. While the man slept, the LORD God took out one of the man's ribs and closed up the opening. Then the LORD God made a woman from the rib, and he brought her to the man.

'At last!' the man exclaimed.

'This one is bone from my bone, and flesh from my flesh! She will be called 'woman,' because she was taken from 'man.''

This explains why a man leaves his father and mother and is joined to his wife, and the two are united into one. Now the man and his wife were both naked, but they felt no shame."—Genesis 2:15-25

A few things stand out to me:

"Help" is a verb, which means it's an action word. A helper isn't sitting around; the helper is *active*. You can see the help.

The definition of help is, "to give or provide what is necessary to to accomplish a task or satisfy a need; contribute strength or means to; render assistance to; cooperate effectively with; aid; assist."

This tells me that God has selected you as a mate to give or provide what is necessary to accomplish a task or satisfy a need to your partner, to contribute strength in your marriage, and to render assistance to.

God has selected you to *help* your spouse in and out of every season. This doesn't change when you don't like him, when you feel like he isn't listening, when you don't feel like he is meeting your needs, when you don't respect him, or anything else based on our feelings.

When we get married we become one flesh and we get the opportunity to fill the voids of each other's weaknesses. Maybe he isn't a strong leader, maybe he is passive, maybe he is not great with money, or maybe he isn't as loving—did you know that God can use you to help, assist, and provide clarity on any area your spouse may be weak in?

When my husband told me that the Lord told him to leave his job three months into getting married, I became our household's income. Prior to this, I never paid any bills in the house and the money that came in from my job was our "fun" money. Cornelius was always very responsible and was very much the "breadwinner" in our home. People would question, "When is he getting a job? When this, and when that?" Well the Lord didn't tell me to quit my job at the time, so I continued to thankfully work remotely for a company that was out of state in a position created specifically for me. I knew that God was using me to *help* pay the bills during that season. My husband wasn't sitting around, playing video games. He would wake up every morning, shower, get dressed, and take his bible, notepad, and laptop to the rooftop of our apartment building to pray and spend time with the Lord. I would watch him spend 8-10 hours a day with the Lord in prayer and in studying.

We didn't realize it at the time, but the Lord was preparing my husband for our church, The Gathering Oasis. He literally had to re-learn everything that he had ever been taught when it came to Jesus. He couldn't depend on past information from our old church or his mama's God; he needed a word from the Lord himself. I recall one day, my husband woke up, put a suit on, and told me that he was going to McDonalds to get a job. I looked at him completely puzzled and told him that God didn't tell him to get a job. I gently reminded him that the Lord is using the job He has given me to provide for our home. It's not my money, it's OUR money.

Was it tough to go through that period? Yes, it was! I respect my husband and I completely believed whatever he told me in regards to our calling, but I had my hard days where I felt the burden of carrying our home financially. I would often think about how much faster we could get out of debt if Cornelius would just get a job. Come on LORD! In the midst of my frustration I heard the Lord, *"Heather, is the job you have yours or Cornelius'?"* Umm, Lord. It's mine. I bring in this amount of money every month. He replied, *"If you want to continue to think that way, I can humble you and take the job away all together. It is I that gave you the job to meet your needs during this season and it's not for you to hang over your husband's head or even charge him for not working. Your husband is in position, but is your heart?"*

Whoa.

My heart was so wrong. I actually thought that I was doing something with my little nine to five and thinking that I was the provider. No, the Lord is our Provider. *He was simply using me to support our family's calling.*

God is our Provider, not my husband. My husband provides spiritual authority to our family and that is much greater than money.

1 Corinthians 11:3 says, "But there is one thing I want you to know: The head of every man is Christ, the head of woman is man, and the head of Christ is God." This tells me that my husband is my spiritual authority and this does not change if my husband isn't working for a season. In our case, the Lord confirmed to me that he shouldn't be working but preparing. So, I was in agreement and we were on the same page. It's important to make sure that you're on the same page and not using

my husband's example as a formula. God specifically told him to not work for that season and again, confirmed it in my spirit.

What about 1 Timothy 5:8? "But if anyone does not provide for his relatives, and especially for members of his household, he has denied the faith and is worse than an unbeliever."

Paul is not directing this command to men only but to anyone, and it doesn't speak directly to working outside the home. A man is a man because he has the foresight to do what is necessary to take care of the needs of his family based on what the Holy Spirit tells him to do as the head of his home. For some it may mean working outside the home, for others it may mean working from home. For some it may mean supporting their wives as they bring in the primary source of income. There are many wives who earn more money than their husbands and are delighted to do so! Will they, either the husband or the wife, be condemned because of it? Of course not!

Contrarily, if you feel like your husband is lazy, refuses to work, and is not only not providing financially, but also not providing spiritual headship, my advice is to not nag him, suggest 40 different things he can do, or even roll your eyes at him daily while saying nothing. Instead, seek to understand the root of your husband's issues. Maybe he is suffering from depression, maybe he is afraid to lead you because you have yet to submit, maybe he is insecure about his calling; whatever the reason, my prayer for you is that you *help* him get through this season. Bashing him and complaining will not motivate him. Instead, take your husband to the Lord and lay him down on the alter of your home. If you are very busy, successful, and you seem like you have it all together, he may feel inferior to that truth. Granted, you cannot change his feelings as only the Lord can heal those areas in his heart but you can still help him get out of this season.

Regardless of what season you are in with your spouse, you get the opportunity to *help*. How cool? The thing about help is that he doesn't need you to try to take over or control him—you are not his mama or his God. As a helpmeet, my husband and I talk about everything and I share my point of view but at the end of the day, *I know that God will hold my husband accountable for his actions.* I also know that my husband is constantly seeking to make the best decision for our family. Did I always feel that way? Definitely not, but I have learned to trust that my husband is doing his best even if it doesn't look that way.

When women confide in me that they feel their husband is leading them down the wrong path, I reiterate that when you said, "I do," you agreed to lovingly respect his headship. Now God would never tell you to submit to anything illegal or immoral, *but in order for him to lead you, you may have to learn to practice relinquishing control.* That means you may have to let your husband fall a couple times as he tries to learn how to lead your family. Grace him by acknowledging the huge responsibility he bares as the head of your home. He is trying to lead you the best that he knows how. He is not perfect, but we must remember that we are not either.

I often talk about the "spirit of shut up" –Or the spirit of "self control." Galatians 5:23 tells us that one of the fruits of the Spirit is temperance, or self control." If I can be honest, there's many times where I have had to stir myself up in the spirit of shut up. Why? Because at times I think that I know how to lead our family and do everything in general. I can be very strong willed and I have this "take-over" personality. Most times, it's not intentional because my husband is a wonderful leader. I am have one of those quick-willed type of personalities. You may feel like you're the same way. I have found that when I shut up, it gives the Holy Spirit a chance to actually speak to my husband. When my mouth is running and complaining while nagging, I miss out on an opportunity for the Holy Spirit to minister to my husband and our situation. This takes great patience because you have to trust that the Holy Spirit is really going to HELP you and work out things for your good. We have to let go of this mindset that says, "if I don't do it, it won't get done!" If your husband says that he has it, *you get the opportunity to let him have it.* God is going to hold him responsible as the leader of your home! Rest in the fact that if you submitted to your husband, it was onto the Lord and not in vain. God honors that submission.

The beauty in marriage is that overtime you will be able to figure out your strengths and weaknesses and you will get to operate in your strengths within your marriage.

For example, I cannot expect for my husband to plan trips for us. It's not in an area of strength for him. I can complain, fuss and wish that he would surprise me with a trip somewhere but he isn't naturally wired to think that way. It's in my nature to plan affordable trips and find amazing hotels, restaurants and things to do while visiting that place. I actually enjoy being the travel agent over our family!

So, how many times have you gotten upset at your husband over an area where he has no strength in?

Well, Heather, He needs to get some strength in that area because this is what I WANT IN A MAN!

So, where did you pick up that mindset? Social media? A movie? A TV show of "what you think you need in a husband?" Is it even biblical? The bible doesn't say anywhere that "Thou Husband should wash thy feet every day and shall shower thou with trips." It says in Ephesians 5:25-26 "Husbands, love your wives, even as Christ also loved the church, and gave Himself for it, that He might sanctify and cleanse it with the washing of the water by the word."

I would rather my husband wash me with the water of the word or push me closer to Jesus than complain about the small things I think he needs to do. Remember that you married that man and said "for better or for worse." And, you cannot change that man. *If he does change temporarily, he will only do it to shut you up, not because he really wants to do that thing.*

Part of marriage is learning to accept your husband for who God made him to be as a man. My husband may not plan trips, but he leads our home so wonderfully. He preaches the word of God with great conviction. He makes sure that he spends time with our family and I never feel second to ministry, our church or anything else. If I compare what he does to what he doesn't do, there's no comparison. And, if you keep focusing on what he doesn't do, *your heart is going to get weary.* Then, you will be tempted to divorce him and run into the arms of a man that will plan a trip but that's only when he actually comes home at night because he is too busy running the streets. See, honey the grass is as green as your perspective.

While watching a documentary on lion prides, I saw that the lioness would go and hunt for food while the male lion would rest. She also took care of the cubs, and again the lion would rest. I'm thinking, "I'm going to need this lion to get up and actually help his lady! He can at least watch the kids! Why does the lioness have to hunt and nurture their cubs?" Then the lioness took the food back to the lion *and* he got to eat first! So not only does she have to go get the food, but she eats last? Wow! Then something really interesting happened—while they were eating they got attacked! I saw the lion spring into action and everything made sense as I watched him protect his pride. I know it seems like you do everything: the cooking, dealing with the kids, and you feel like you're constantly tending to things while your husband is resting, but who gets attacked if they are the head? Our husbands. They carry a heavier yoke than us because they hold the responsibility of our spiritual headship. So give your guy a break.

I know he may not do everything you want him to do, but I want to encourage you to find ways to be thankful for what he does well. Maybe he is a hard worker, he serves at church, he always comes home to you at night, or he's wonderful with the kids—regardless of what he's done wrong, focus on what he does right. I don't know about you, but I don't want to be a single mama of two babies while sharing custody of our children. I don't believe anybody wants to do those things alone or separated. Divorce doesn't happen "all of a sudden." It's little by little—a little disrespect here, a little arguing here, a little bashing there. I believe that Satan seeks to plant bad seeds into your life and marriage and he would love for you to roll your neck, be rebellious, loud, unforgiving and and to never submit. It's easy to rebel in your marriage, but it takes great strength to submit to your husband as unto the Lord, especially when we feel they don't deserve it. I truly don't believe the Lord asks us how we "feel" about submission or if we think our spouse deserves it. I'm confident that we don't deserve the grace of Jesus when we sin but He still gives it to us. Let's give some grace to our spouse.

I don't know your husband and I don't know what he's done or doesn't do, but I believe that you were given to him by God to *help* him to be a better man. Pray for him like crazy, trust that God can change him, and work on changing the only person you can change—you.

Chapter 13

Being the Leader

My wife and I are firm believers in the traditional family, which we define as a loving husband and a submitted wife. We believe, as it is explained in 1 Corinthians 11:3 and Ephesians 5:23, that the husband is the head and authority of the household. This does not mean he is domineering or that she does not have a voice but that there is order and structure in the home. It is commonly said that anything with two heads is a monster—someone has to bow their knee in submission. As my wife has written previously, *submission it is not something to be feared but is proof of great strength and is for your protection.* There are times when both of you will need to submit to one with another and this allows for complete symmetry and peace within the home. It is important to understand the significance of order in order to value and respect the position of leadership.

Ephesians 5:22-33 tells us that wives should respect their husband and husbands should respect their wife.

They do this as unto the Lord. It mirrors the relationship between Christ and the Church. When a man and women are married, they become one flesh. The Church submits itself to Christ as the wife submits herself to her husband in all things (Ephesians 5:22-24). This means there are no other competing interests. She is to be inclined to yield to her husband's authority and is predisposed to follow his leadership. Christ humbly served the Church. If wives are to take their cue from the submissiveness of the Church towards Christ, then the husband should take his role of serving his wife very seriously. In fact, Christ laid down His life for His church. John 10:11, John 15:13, and 1 John 3:16 all speak about the love of Christ laying His life down for His Church. This means He paid the ultimate sacrifice. He gave everything up for them. As a husband, that must be a priority for his wife. She should know that she is loved because her husband is willing to lay down His life for her. And because she is Spirit-filled, she will not seek to take advantage of his sacrifice.

Christ made the way easy for the Church. He presented Her with a way out of sin. Husbands practice that in their marriage. They seek to make the easy for their wife. They recognize that she is the weaker vessel (1 Peter 3:7). He recognizes that while she is the weaker vessel, it doesn't make her his slave. She's valuable and precious to him; therefore, he protects her as such.

If we haven't already, lets make it crystal clear that the enemy is after your marriage. He does not want you and your spouse to last till death do you both part. He desires for the two of you to divorce, which causes unneeded and unwanted problems in the household for future generations. He is very crafty in his approach to divide the two of you but God calls for us to be unified. He will seek to get you and your spouse away from one another long enough to fill your minds with unflattering thoughts, which creates tension and questions loyalty. He will continue to do this until you grow in hatred toward one another. He will confuse and convince the both of you to cut off communication, hindering your intimacy. You will begin to confide in others close to you, creating intimate relationships with people other than your spouse—opening the door to infidelity.

The enemy slithered up to Eve in the Garden of Eden and convinced her to eat of the tree that God forbade them to eat. He convinced her to defy God, undermine her husband's headship, and commit an act that was forbidden. In fact, he was disrespectful to even go to Eve instead of Adam but he knew exactly what he was doing. Adam was the one who was given the instructions from God in Genesis 2:16-17. He was fully aware of God's orders, and he should have been the one the enemy questioned; however, his plan was to go after the weaker of the two. The enemy went to the woman to dissuade her of what we can expect was told to her by her husband since she was not yet created when God instructed Adam about the tree. Adam was created first, which alone denotes headship. The respectful thing to do would have been to speak with him first before addressing his wife. That did not happen because the enemy does not acknowledge order or anything ordained by the Father. The enemy knew that he could manipulate the woman's emotions easier than convincing Adam to go against what he knew to be true. But as the wife ate, so did her husband and what followed was guilt, shame, and regret. *Rest assured that the enemy will do all he can to go through the woman if he cannot directly influence the man.*

The enemy has a plan to cut off the head of the house. In referring to the man as the "head of the household" I don't want it to be confused with Titus 2:3-5 where it refers to the woman as the keeper of the home. It is important for me to mention that the woman has a biblical responsibility to keep the home, which means she guards it. Most notably, she guards the *peace* of the home. She sets the tone, provides structure, and maintains a biblical routine. She reduces conflict, enforces principles, and restores whatever is broken or lacking. She sets a great example of honor towards her husband so the children will practice and emulate it in their relationship with their father and towards the Lord. She makes it a place of comfort for the entire family.

You may ask what the man is supposed to do if the woman is called to keep the home. Traditionally, his role has been to work hard so there is a home to be kept but our society has changed a lot over the years. Women have lost much of their desire to keep the home or are never introduced to the concept of what that means. Today women are commonly encouraged to be successful outside of the home while ignoring the spiritual condition of their family. Let's not leave out the single mothers that are forced to provide physically and emotionally. The Gospel is a message of liberation, but with righteous liberation comes boundaries. While it is socially acceptable for women to be great successes out of the home, they should not ignore or discount the importance of keeping it as they are instructed in the Word of God.

The enemy will look to attack the man first. The man is vital to the strength of the family; therefore, if he dethrones the king then the kingdom is open for takeover. As my wife explained, when predators seek to attack a lion pride, they wait until the alpha is absent or distracted. When a rogue lion seeks to take over the pride, he goes to dethrone the alpha lion and fights him until he is victorious. After he wins, he kills the cubs to make sure the defeated lion's lineage is no more, and he humbles any rebellious lionesses. If they do not submit, then they die as well. In 1 Peter 5:8 we see that the enemy is like a lion seeking those he can devour. He knows his easier targets are the women and children. All he has to do is remove the man from the equation or convince him that he cannot fight back.

He desires to cut the head off the man so the body is rendered useless. Christ is the head of the husband, the husband is the head of his wife, and the wife is the keeper of the home. His first goal is to dethrone Christ as king and authority in your household—he wants to render His words useless and of no effect. This removes a standard, and there is chaos wherever a standard is lacking. Consider a household where there are no rules—it's chaotic, right? That is what happens when the Word of God is not the final authority your home. When Christ's instructions aren't the authority then you and your husband are free to make up any rules as you all see fit and you probably won't agree.

Christ's words are righteous and He is the righteous standard. When your words are void of Christ, they are destructive and damaging. As the leader, the man must make it his responsibility to gather his family together and proclaim, like Joshua, that he and his family will serve the Lord (Joshua 24:15). He makes it clear that service to the Lord is both personal and collective. He states that as long as he is the authority in the home, everyone will serve the Lord.

After removing the authority of the Lord from your home, the enemy will seek to remove the presence of physical leadership—the husband. This is the current landscape of many homes today. The men are so preoccupied with everything outside their home that they don't see the chaos going on within it. The enemy doesn't mind if the husband and father is ambitious, especially if it means he has to sacrifice his family time. He will seek to remove the man from the home, convince him that he is unwanted, try to emasculate him, and make him feel like he is worthless. He will do everything he possibly can to cut off the headship of the man, which leaves the family in chaos. Many households have grown comfortable with no man being present and active; however, the husband and father's presence will always be important. It is vital! The father and husband provides protection, provision, identity, affirmation, and acceptance. Our children show the results of present and active fathers, or lack thereof. His leadership must be seen and worth emulating.

To be the leader is not an easy task. It means you have to bear the burdens of your family. Being the leader means you hold them up in prayer and are willing to carefully teach them the truth as the priest of your home. Your leadership isn't domineering or by the use of fear, it is loving, patient, and kind; as Christ loves the church, so the man is to love his wife. Like Christ, he seeks to make her way easy and eases her of her burdens. He is forgiving and merciful, gentle and humble. He doesn't seek to demean his wife. He loves her so much that like Christ, he doesn't seek to harm her. He recognizes that his wife is more precious than his own life, and he is willing to give up his life that she might live. The leader provides direction and vision. He is willing to seek the Lord concerning his family and the way they should go. He manages his children and his household well so he can qualify himself for a position in the church. He should be active in his church community and should lead his family in attending service regularly. He leads with dignity and honor, recognizing that his actions must be held accountable. He cannot afford to let his family down. He doesn't lead with sarcasm or anger, but with a servant's heart as he is honored to fulfill the responsibility as the leader of the home.

Heather runs a women's ministry on her own, but she graciously allows me the honor of overseeing it. This means I oversee the gifts God has given her and I help to make sure ministry doesn't consume her. It is already enough to be a wife and mother, especially knowing that I am a handful by myself. She receives invitations to speak often, but we discuss all of them. She lets me know the ones she would like to approve, then allows me the honor of praying over them. I refuse to send my wife out in this dangerous world to a place I'm not sure of. I will schedule whatever I need to in order to make sure her entire way is easy. Overseeing the ministry is important to me, and I'm honored to be married to a wife who understands the importance of headship. We have been around married couples where the woman took over the position of leadership. Her way was the only way and she was the proverbial 'neck that turned the head.' She did not consult with her husband about her speaking engagements and went wherever she felt was acceptable. Her husband made excuses for his lack of involvement, citing her ability to make her own decisions. While my wife is fully capable of making her own decisions, I take my headship seriously. For my wife to do something without my knowledge is a lack of righteous oversight and leadership, and a poor reflection of my ability to lead.

Not only do I oversee my wife's ministry, but I also oversee her relationships. I'm not in the business of telling my wife who to be friends with, but I let her know if I see something in one of the women she befriends. *We submit to one another in this way as my wife assists me in discerning my friends as well.* I do not desire for my wife to be around gossipy, nagging women. We understand that whoever she is around could influence her. I encourage my wife to be around women who edify one another, are successful in their home, and love their husbands. My goal in overseeing her relationships is to help provide balance. I desire to help her prioritize her responsibilities so she doesn't burn out or become overwhelmed with the cares of this world. It's important to me that she has days where she rests without working.

It's so easy to become disconnected in a world filled with distractions. Everything is pulling on you and straining your marriage: Social media, television, school, work, and everything else that demands our attention. Once you acknowledge the distractions, it's essential to find time to reconnect with heartfelt communication and physical intimacy. My wife and I find cost efficient ways to travel so we can have time alone. Before many of these ways became available to us, we opted to drive to the bordering state, visit a mall to look around, walk around a park, find a restaurant to eat, and spend the night in a hotel within our budget. It doesn't have to be expensive or extravagant; it is the act of recharging that matters. The focus should be on the man desiring to lead his wife in finding relaxation, reconnection, and an escape from the routine of life.

It is also wise for the husband to lead his wife in prayer and study of the Scriptures because the Word of God should be the standard in the home. My wife and I had to realize the importance of having, knowing, and understanding the righteous standard early on in our marriage. We argued constantly, and it did not seem like either of us wanted to submit or be the one to give in. We just kept arguing over and over again. The standard in our home became so vitally important because it became the way by which all arguments ceased. We both agreed that the Word of God had to be the final authority. If we were perplexed about the meaning of what was written, we would reach out to mutually agreed upon advisors for our marriage. These were couples that we honored enough to have minister into our lives. Having a holy standard in our home cut down on the disagreements substantially. At the end of the day, I knew I needed to be more graceful with my wife, and she was challenged to be more merciful with me. The standard showed us ourselves. It was like looking into a mirror. What was important was that we both agreed that it was the final authority in our home.

In order to apply it and see its power, we had to be dedicated in learning and knowing the Word of God. I, as the husband and leader, needed to make sure we understood it. I took it upon myself to learn whatever was needed, to read whatever books necessary, and listen to wise counsel so I was willing and able to stand as the priest in my home. I meet many men who feel very insecure about taking on the priestly role because they feel like their wife is far more knowledgeable about scripture, their understanding is lacking, and/or they don't want the burden of it. The men who do not want the burden of it would rather leave the teaching of Scripture to their pastor or clergyman. *While this can be great to be under righteous leadership, the husband must never leave another man to be solely responsible for the spiritual health of his family.* He should hear the words spoken, study them, and show himself approved. Failing to do so could result in his wife and family receiving false information.

Attending church, reading the scriptures at home, praying together, and being edified spiritually allows for the couple to be built up so they can withstand the onslaught of the enemy. When they are tried and tested, their faith proves to be real and solid—built on a solid foundation. Their issues aren't able to pierce through their shield of faith and their sword of the Spirit is sharp. They're able to fight and withstand the enemy. They're able to deny temptation when it comes. They are ready for battle! *A couple that attends church separately and serves separately tends to grow separately.* Heather and I enjoy attending conferences together, as well as apart. We don't usually accompany one another on those trips, but we are aware of the teachers before going and we discuss what we learned once we return. We share the truths with one another. This keeps us both involved in one another's personal growth and helps us grow together.

If your house isn't orderly then it's in chaos. Unfortunately, I see chaotic homes all time as a pastor. A precedence must be set to spend quality time as a unit, while prioritizing our responsibilities outside of the home. If our children don't see an example set by their parents, they will look to outside influences to determine what's right and wrong, and by the time we get our head out of our own distractions, it will be too late.

Order in the home includes: the husband loving his wife as Christ loves the Church (Ephesians 5:25); the leader of the home managing his household well, which includes keeping his children under control (1 Timothy 3:4); maintaining a righteous standard in the home that proclaims with an unwavering confidence that the house will serve the Lord (Joshua 24:15); requiring that the children live honorable and respectful lives that leaves a good name for their parents on earth (Exodus 20:12); not sparing the rod of discipline, driving out any rebellion in the children (Proverbs 13:24); a wife that is respectful and submissive to her husband, creating an example for her children to follow (Titus 2:4-5.)

God gives us a standard of leadership and order in His Word that should never be ignored. It is our responsibility to study it and apply it so that we may experience the fruit of Holy Spirit in our marriages and in our households.

Chapter 14

Worth the Fight

You learn to abuse whatever you haven't learned to value. A prudent manufacturer doesn't discount his product to make it acceptable for the public; instead, he explains the value of the product so they understand the cost. Value doesn't beg, and it doesn't drop its price to be accepted. It's important to understand the value of something so it isn't abused or treated as if it's something common. Marriage is valuable. *Your* marriage is valuable.

I did not understand this principle when Heather and I first got married. I was careless with my words and tried to wound her with them. Yes, my insecurity drove me to wound the one I shared my life with in hopes that she would hurt like I was hurting. Most times my wife was not the issue but she was the closest person to me. Like many people, I chose to take my frustrations out on the person who was around me the most. Looking back, I wish I understood my wife's worth and value. I wish I understood my marriage's worth and value.

Understanding it would have allowed me to treat my marriage as if it were valuable. Not understanding the value opened the door for me to abuse it.

I started working at 15 years old. It wasn't the most honorable job, but it was work nonetheless. It was tough to juggle work with school, but I learned many valuable lessons and I was determined to save as much money as I could so that I could buy a car. I hated to ask my parents for anything, and that included a ride to school, so it was a great moment for me once I finally found a car I could afford! I was able to purchase my 1994 Nissan Sentra with cash. To others, the car was not anything to smile about, but it was worth its weight in gold to me. I was at the car wash every other day wiping it down and vacuuming the inside because it meant a lot to me. I understood its worth and value. I knew the hard work it took to earn the money to purchase it. I could remember the patience, diligence, and discipline it took to save the money I was earning. Although the car was worthless to others, it meant the world to me and my actions towards the car showed how much I valued it. I did not ascribe that same value to my marriage, and my actions were the proof.

When your marriage is worth fighting for, you will act like it. You will be willing to defend your spouse at all costs, willing to defend the peace in your home from anyone or anything that threatens to steal it, and willing to defend your marriage. These actions show that you truly value your marriage and that it is worth fighting for.

Worth The Fight

Imagine someone is trying to break into your home. You are alerted from an alarm system, and you can see the burglar from a camera that is setup outside. There are many things you could do in that situation, but I will focus on two: fight back or be taken advantage of. If you choose to stand at the door and allow the burglar to have his way with you, you are refusing to fight back against the onslaught of the enemy. You can stand there and watch as he steals everything you have worked hard for, or you can prepare for a fight!

On the other hand, when the door swings open you could pounce on the burglar, which starts a tussle. There are times when it looks like he might be getting the best of you, but you refuse to quit. You keep fighting back until the enemy realizes he is bested. He gets up from the fight and flees. You are tired and exhausted, but you're victorious! The enemy stole nothing, deceived no one, and did not ruin anything. He will think twice before trying to come in your house again. He is fully aware that you are a fighter, and you won't just quit. The same principles apply when the enemy is after your marriage.

I know couples who sit idly by while the enemy has his way with them. *They don't open their mouths to pray, take time to fast, or stop to praise the Lord.* Instead, they give up on one another while the enemy terrorizes their home. He confuses their language, making it difficult for them to communicate—one wants to talk while the other just stays silent. The bedroom is a symbol of covenant intimacy, so Satan strives to make it so uncomfortable that all intimacy ceases. He tears through every room of the house, including those of the children by making them believe they are the cause of mommy and daddy's issues. He tries to convince them that they aren't loved, while stealing any ounce of peace that was once in the home. He divides and seeks to conquer the entire family with the goal of divorce. This creates dysfunction that will ultimately affect future generations, beginning with their children.

What's even more troubling is that the enemy isn't fighting against one. **He is fighting both of you so the battle to survive shouldn't be lopsided!** In some scenarios it can even seem like one spouse is working with and for the enemy, while the other is in the spiritual fight of their life. Then there is the scenario where the enemy has forcefully broken down the door, but there's no opposition for him because the couple is fighting against one another. Instead of engaging in battle, Satan walks right by them with a huge smile on his face. He is joyful that he doesn't have to fight. **Why? Because the couple is fighting each other instead of fighting together!** The enemy doesn't care what they are fighting about, all he is concerned with is getting them distracted so he can have his way in their home. He simply wants an open door.

While they argue Satan slips upstairs to the children's rooms. He slithers into your daughter's room and whispers into her ear that she is not as pretty as the other girls at school. He tries to convince her that she doesn't look like the women she sees on television. He seeks to create a battle in her heart that is so intense that every man who seeks to love her will feel her wrath and rage. He tries to convince her that she just isn't enough and that she is worthless. He knows that if he can convince her that she isn't valuable then she will abuse her body and sell herself short to any man that comes along. Satan slips over into your son's room and tries to convince him that he needs to be like the men he sees on television and those he listens to through his earphones. He works hard to convince him that he is worthless and not capable of being anyone of value. He works hard at getting him entangled in lustful activity that eventually ruins his character. Your son attempts to validate himself in the streets by following the wrong crowd or in the bedroom with a woman he isn't married to. The enemy is able to have a field day with your children because you and your spouse are too busy fighting one another to notice the enemy that sleeps in your bed. No, he doesn't leave daily and return on occasion. He makes your most intimate place his residence; he stays there.

The enemy continues to do this over and over again until you finally come to the conclusion that your marriage is worth fighting for. Realize that a fight for your marriage is a fight for your family! The enemy is after your family. He seeks to destroy your linage, disrupt your peace, and confuse your orderly home. He wants to cause chaos and rebellion. He loves that you and your spouse don't attend church regularly because he knows that your marriage will lack accountability, proper teaching, and spiritual guidance. He also doesn't mind if you attend church service but never act on what you hear. What good is it to go to school but never use the degree? In the same way, what good is it to attend a church service but never act on the Word of God? What good is it to know about faith but live like you don't; to know about love but live with hatred in your heart; to know about grace but treat it as if it was something common? You don't scare him because you're a pew-sitter! The enemy would have no choice but to flee if you were armed with the Word of God as a Spirit-filled believer saturated in Jesus Christ!

I had to come to a place where I realized that my marriage was worth my willingness to fight. I will never forget the day my wife looked at me and said, *"I just haven't felt pretty lately."* Those words pierced my heart. Why? Because it was my job to reassure my wife of what I know she should be confident in. I failed to do that because of my own insecurities. My failure to combat the voice of the enemy with the Word of God was causing insecurity to grow in my wife. I needed to be there to fight with my wife against that mental battle. It is in moments like these where I learn the importance of fighting for my marriage.

In a fight you must always be ready. Ephesians 6:10-18 tells us to be strong in the Lord and in His mighty power. We are to put on the entire armor of God in preparation for war. We must make sure our feet are prepared, breastplate fastened, helmet secure, belt tightened, and our sword sharp! There is an enemy seeking to destroy your household! How long will you allow him to have his way in your home? Satan would love for you to believe this, but please understand that your enemy is not your spouse. These same verses tell us that we prepare ourselves for battle because our enemy is coming with a battalion to fight. He is coming with many weapons but they cannot pierce the armor of God! Hallelujah. We do not fight against flesh and blood. There are spiritual principalities and rulers of darkness that seek to ruin your home. How long will you allow them to stay there?

If you find yourself in a situation where you feel you are fighting alone, STAND AND FIGHT! Why are you afraid to fight alone? We both know you shouldn't have to do it alone, but your spouse has been taken captive for the enemy's purpose.

I've seen people taken hostage by these rulers of darkness and perversion. It was like they were a totally different person, while doing things I never would expect of them. They weren't the partying type, but they found themselves out all night and arriving into work with a hangover. A wife of a captured husband cried on my wife's shoulder as she told us about her husband cheating with another woman. It was breaking her. Heather cried with her for a minute, sat back, looked her in the eyes, and told her, "Girl, fight for your marriage! It's worth fighting for!" The woman wiped her eyes, we prayed together, and she left our office. When we saw her seven months later, she had a huge smile on her face.

She told us that she and her husband had reconciled and were working on their marriage. From the outside looking in it seemed like their marriage was over. He had already found a divorce attorney and was telling everyone that he was done with her, but their story wasn't over. When my wife asked what she was doing while her husband was still in his rebellious stage, she responded, "I was praying and fasting! I decided to fight for my marriage because it's worth fighting for!" She refused to quit, cave in, or allow the enemy to have his way in their home. She stood boldly on the Word of God, and he fled away from her marriage.

We all have to fight for our marriages. There are so many things in the world competing for our time, affection, and attention. We have to fight against ambition, pornography, inappropriate conversations, overindulgence in sports, greed in our spending, and many other conniving distractions of the enemy. There are a multitude of ways the enemy seeps into our homes whether it be through what we watch and read, or through the music we listen to. His goal is to knock your door down, divide, and conquer. Be mindful of what plays in your home, who comes in, and where you and your spouse are receiving guidance. Protect your marriage in the same way the Lord instructs us to guard our hearts. Guard every entrance with vigilance!

Your marriage is worth fighting for! Matthew 19:6 tells us that we should never allow for any mortal being or thing to tear apart that which God has put together. Your vows have been spoken; your words heard by God. Don't allow anyone or anything to separate the two of you.

Worth The Fight

Identify the enemy, and fight! Because your marriage is worth it.

Bonus Chapter

Divorce Proofing your Marriage

1. I can't change my spouse, only God can do that. Your job is to pray.
2. Don't freak out when your spouse tells you crazy stories from the gym, when he/she went paintballing, water rafting on a girls trip or in general. You want your spouse to share everything with you and they will not if you get overly emotional, dramatic and overreact. #Friendship
3. Marriage is a journey. So you married someone who doesn't have your deal breakers? Get ready to go on a journey!
4. Be patient. You're both growing. #Grace
5. Shut up. Yup. There's no point in arguing because we aren't divorcing. Choose your battles. Pursue peace like crazy in your home, put on your big girl & big boy pants and act like Christian adults. #Love

6. Protect your marriage. You and your spouse are one flesh and you should want to be seen on one accord. Be each other's number one fans. Don't share your arguments with people who will hold onto it long after you've made up. #Protection

7. Don't bring up the past. It's behind you for a reason. Move on. #Grace

8. If your spouse is saying a concern, listen. They know you best and believe what they are saying. #Mirror

9. Learn to be content broke or with money. If you're ever evicted, be committed to being homeless together in a tent on the street. Cuddling. #Mine

10. Husbands— love your wife like Christ loves the church. Wives— submit to your Husbands as unto the Lord. He's your leader. God honors you because you honor him.

11. Be flexible in making time for each other. If your schedules get overcrowded, be intentional about cancelling some things in order to have quality family time. #MarriageGodsWay

12. Use discernment when bringing up issues—there is a time and place to present your concerns. Don't let emotions talk you into making every issue an urgent argument.

13. You don't have to argue every time you get upset. Choose your battles! Choose peace for your home.

14. Date each other. Make it a priority.

15. Take divorce out of the conversation. Do not bring it up again.

16. Get around other godly marriages. Make it a priority to attend at least one marriage retreat every year. It's a worthwhile investment.

Marriage and Family Pledge

My wife and I stand together in the defense of marriage and the family. We are united in our faith and allegiance to Jesus Christ. We believe family is a very important cell of society and social order; therefore, we will seek to cherish the honored institution.

We will fight together for our marriage and for the peace in our home. We vow to teach and raise our children in the truth and admonition of the Lord. We vow to be patient and honest with one another. We are gentle and graceful in our responses. We will continue to work on our communication with one another. We are the strength we need for each other, and Jesus Christ is the foundation of our union.

We vow to love each other unconditionally, to support each other in our goals, to honor and respect one another, to cry and laugh with each other, and to cherish one another as long as we both shall live. We vow to be understanding and trust in one another completely. Based on 2 Corinthians 5:17, we are new creations. The old things have passed away. We are living a new life from this moment forward. We refuse to hold the past against one another. Instead we choose to be graceful and merciful. Based on Ephesians 4:32, we choose to forgive one another as Christ has forgiven us.

We stand united. Nothing or no one can tamper with our union! We are stronger together, and our future is brighter than our past. Our marriage is worth the fight. Our family is worth the fight. We are worth the fight. We vow to fight together.

_____   _____
         Husband   Wife

Notes

Gary D Chapman, *The Five Love Languages: The Secret to Love that Lasts* (Chicago: Northfield Publishing, 2010)

All dictionary definitions are taken from *Merriam-Webster.com*. 2016.